Ethics and Professionalism in Forensic Anthropology

Ethics and Professionalism in Forensic Anthropology

Nicholas V. Passalacqua
Western Carolina University, Cullowhee, NC, United States

Marin A. Pilloud
University of Nevada, Reno, NV, United States

ELSEVIER

ACADEMIC PRESS
An imprint of Elsevier

Academic Press is an imprint of Elsevier
125 London Wall, London EC2Y 5AS, United Kingdom
525 B Street, Suite 1800, San Diego, CA 92101-4495, United States
50 Hampshire Street, 5th Floor, Cambridge, MA 02139, United States
The Boulevard, Langford Lane, Kidlington, Oxford OX5 1GB, United Kingdom

British Library Cataloguing-in-Publication Data
A catalogue record for this book is available from the British Library

Library of Congress Cataloging-in-Publication Data
A catalog record for this book is available from the Library of Congress

ISBN: 978-0-12-812065-1

Publisher: John Fedor
Acquisition Editor: Elizabeth Brown
Editorial Project Manager: Timothy Bennett
Production Project Manager: Mohana Natarajan
Cover Designer: Vicky Pearson

Typeset by MPS Limited, Chennai, India

CONTENTS

PREFACE

Forensic anthropology, like all the forensic sciences, is undergoing a period of standardization and validation. However, thus far little attention is being given to: how forensic anthropology functions as a profession, requisite qualifications to be a forensic anthropologist, or ethical considerations within the field. We feel that it is critically important to fully address these issues now for the discipline to make positive forward progress. After discussions between the authors, as well as with other professionals and students in forensic anthropology, we decided the best way to start a conversation and get others thinking about the professional and ethical practice of forensic anthropology was to create this volume. As such, we have attempted to draw attention to some of the more pressing issues within forensic anthropology from a professional and ethical standpoint.

In a practical sense we cover issues relating to accreditation, certification, casework, peer review, legal concerns in studying humans, and expert witness testimony. Beyond these practical issues we also address scientific integrity, misconduct, bias, ethical publishing, discrimination, harassment, and promoting diversity within the field. This book is designed to serve as an introduction to ethics and professionalism within the context of forensic anthropology. We present the reader with an overview of the current state of forensic anthropology as a professional discipline, with a primary focus on forensic anthropology in the United States, although international perspectives are considered as well. This discussion covers topics that are important for forensic anthropologists to understand, yet, are rarely discussed in a professional or systematic way. Therefore forensic anthropologists may be unaware of many of the concepts presented within this volume, and of their ethical and professional obligations in various settings.

While we have attempted to provide guidelines for moving forward on each of these topics; we also realized that acceptance and enforcement of any guidelines requires the involvement of various professional organizations (e.g., the AAFS, OSAC, etc.). We argue throughout this book that professional organizations need to be at the forefront of this charge and this volume is meant to serve as an outline to start the process. We do not expect this treatment to be the last word in these topics; on the contrary, we truly hope to spark a dialogue surrounding these issues and highlight their importance within the discipline. We are excited and optimistic about the future of forensic anthropology and we welcome the opportunity to discuss these and other issues important to the practice of our discipline.

ACKNOWLEDGEMENT

The authors thank the following individuals for their feedback, comments, and reviews to various parts of this volume: Eric Bartelink, Jonathan Bethard, Thomas Holland, Cheryl Hunter, Alex Klales, Kate Lesciotto, Dennis O'Rourke, Casey S. Philbin, Christopher Rainwater, Vincent Sava, Kate Spradley, MariaTeresa Tersigni-Tarrant, P Willey, and Katie Zejdlik. Also thanks to the attendees of the 2016 annual meeting of the Mountain, Desert & Coastal Forensic Anthropologists where we presented some early aspects of this volume. Thanks are also due to the program organizers (Kristen Broehl, Jessica Curry, Kelsie Hart, and Valerie Sgheiza) and attendees of the 2017 California State University, Chico Forensics Conference where we discussed various ethical issues in biological anthropology. We also thank Graciela Cabana and Jennifer Wagner for clarifying issues relating to the American Association of Physical Anthropologists ethical stance. Finally, we are grateful to our editors at Academic Press, Joslyn T. Chaiprasert-Paguio, Elizabeth Brown, and Tim Bennett for their patience and guidance.

CHAPTER 1

Introduction to Professionalism, Ethics, and Forensic Anthropology

While considered an important aspect of education in medical school, professionalism and ethics are not subjects frequently discussed in forensic anthropology classrooms. Applied anthropology programs are more likely to offer ethics as part of their education; however, ethics are not frequently found as a required part of anthropology programs (Trotter, 2009). This general trend is also reflected in the literature as there are few publications that deal with professionalism or ethics within the context of forensic anthropology (see France, 2012; Walsh-Haney and Lieberman, 2005).

This lack of focus on ethics does not mean that forensic anthropologists are unethical. Rather the lack of material on these subjects likely results from the relatively young nature of forensic anthropology and the fact that even now much of forensic anthropology is rather disjointed and lacks professional standards. While there are numerous ethical codes to which many forensic anthropologists adhere as part of their professional memberships (e.g., those of the American Academy of Forensic Sciences [AAFS], the American Association of Physical Anthropologists [AAPA], the American Board of Forensic Anthropology [ABFA])[1], there are also many individuals practicing forensic anthropology, or using the title "forensic anthropologist" without qualifications or any of these professional affiliations.

The goal for this volume echoes that of a similar volume, *Ethics and the Profession of Anthropology* (Fluehr-Lobban, 2003:xiii), in that we aim to begin the "dialogue for ethically conscious practice" of forensic anthropology. We will discuss current and best practices on a number of topics, and outline the need for professional and ethical standards within the field. The discussion we present is meant to be

[1]The reader may also refer to Appendix A for a full list of acronyms.

Ethics and Professionalism in Forensic Anthropology. DOI: https://doi.org/10.1016/B978-0-12-812065-1.00001-4

beyond any specific set of state or federal regulations that may guide different types of analyses, testing, reporting, or handling of remains. Instead, we explore the role of the forensic anthropologist and the ethical boundaries of working with human remains within the medicolegal system. While we discuss current and best practices on a number of topics, we do not intend for this volume to be an exhaustive reference of proper conduct in all circumstances, nor do we anticipate all forensic anthropologists to agree with the issues presented here. Additionally, we will not discuss the history of ethics in anthropology generally, nor touch on anthropological issues outside of those directly relating to forensic anthropology. Rather, we hope this volume will *start* the discussion about the ethical practice of forensic anthropology and bring to light different approaches to professionalism and the practice of forensic anthropology.

INTRODUCTION TO PROFESSIONALISM

In very general terms, a profession is a paid occupation, a professional is someone who belongs to a certain profession, and professionalism is conduct associated with a particular profession. All of these definitions fail to address what constitutes the *qualifications* and *appropriate behaviors* that are requisite for a given profession. What constitutes professionalism can be defined according to various disciplines. Within forensic anthropology, and the forensic sciences in general, there is a dearth of literature on the definition of these terms. Perhaps the most relevant to forensic anthropology would also be that outlined for medical professionals. Generally, within this literature a professional is someone who possesses a body of special knowledge, practices within an ethical framework, and fulfills a societal need (Pellegrino, 2002). Within the context of forensic anthropology, we can extend this to include a professional as someone who is a properly trained subject-matter expert who will analyze a case without a conflict of interest, and will follow an appropriate code of conduct. Throughout this book we outline more specific definitions of professionalism (Chapter 2: The Need for Professional Ethics) and the specific practices and behaviors that are requisite of a professional forensic anthropologist (Chapter 4: Defining the Role of the Forensic Anthropologist; Chapter 5: The use of Human Subjects in Forensic Anthropology Research; Chapter 6: Reporting and Testifying in Forensic Anthropology; and Chapter 7: Discrimination and Harassment in Forensic Anthropology).

INTRODUCTION TO ETHICS

Ethics is a branch of philosophy that is concerned with morality and behaviors (i.e., conduct) that can be considered right or wrong based on different criteria (Bowen, 2009). There are traditionally three fields of inquiry within the field of ethics: metaethics, normative ethics, and applied ethics (Attfield, 2012). Within this treatment, we will focus on normative ethics, to establish standards and guidelines for behavior within forensic anthropology. Here we define ethics as guidelines for the behavior of individuals within a specific profession or discipline. An ethical code is a set of rules dealing with ethical issues that have been agreed upon by a professional body (e.g., the AAFS). Different professional organizations may have different ethical codes, but all are used in order to ensure members avoid unprofessional behaviors and thus maintain the credibility of the profession and professional organization.

Morals and moral codes are similar to ethics and ethical codes; however, they vary in a few key ways. Most importantly, morals are not *professionalized*; meaning they are not typically written down or agreed upon by all parties. Further, because morals are not professionally recognized, they often lead to disagreement about their validity or applicability as each individual may have their own personal interpretation regarding a moral rule. Of note is that all "ethical codes draw to some extent on the generally accepted moral values of the culture in which the ethical codes are developed; but moral principles are, in themselves, insufficient to govern action" (Barnett, 2001:14). While Chapter 3, Current Ethical Guidelines and a Theory of Ethics, will deal specifically with different ethical codes relating to forensic anthropology, it is important to remember that each profession may have its own ethical codes, which function uniquely in order to promote positive impacts from its practitioners on society.

INTRODUCTION TO FORENSIC ANTHROPOLOGY

Forensic anthropology is "the application of anthropological method and theory to matters of legal concern, particularly those that relate to the recovery and analysis of the human skeleton" (Christensen et al., 2014:2). For this volume we will take the typical North American approach to forensic anthropology, that is combining the systematic search and recovery of evidence and remains (*forensic archaeology*) and the analysis of biological, usually dental and skeletal materials (*forensic anthropology*) into the singular discipline of forensic anthropology. However, we do acknowledge that different regions have different approaches to the practice of forensic anthropology. In the United Kingdom for example, forensic archaeology is considered a separate discipline, and training in forensic archaeology typically occurs as an entirely detached program from forensic anthropological (i.e., skeletal) training. Further, in much of Europe, analyses typically considered to fall under the purview of forensic anthropology are performed by doctors of forensic medicine, and forensic archaeology is performed by individuals trained in archaeology. While we plan to focus on the North American approach to forensic anthropology, when relevant, we will touch on various international models as well.

Forensic anthropology, like all forensic sciences, can be thought of as employing rigorous scientific methodology combined with forensic (meaning legal) documentary paperwork (largely for the purposes of traceability and transparency). Functionally, what this means is that despite what television shows lead us to believe, forensic anthropology, or any forensic science, is actually a tedious endeavor requiring significant amounts of paperwork, documentation, and bureaucracy for even simple analyses and reporting.

When it comes to any of the forensic sciences the importance of the scientific method cannot be discounted. The scientific method requires that scientists observe different phenomena using valid methods, and to use the results of these observations to draw conclusions about what was observed. "Critical to the scientific method is that the scientist's conclusions can be verified by other scientists. This requires that the methods and processes that underlie a scientist's opinion are available to another scientist for review" (Barnett, 2001:18). Further, science must follow the scientific method as illustrated in Fig. 1.1. As the reader is well aware, this process begins with an observation that is followed by topical research that helps in the development of a testable statement, i.e., a hypothesis. The hypothesis leads to the formulation of a research experiment in which the hypothesis can be falsified. If the hypothesis can be falsified the researcher rejects it and formulates a separate testable hypothesis to begin the process again. If repeated experiments fail to falsify a hypothesis the beginnings of a

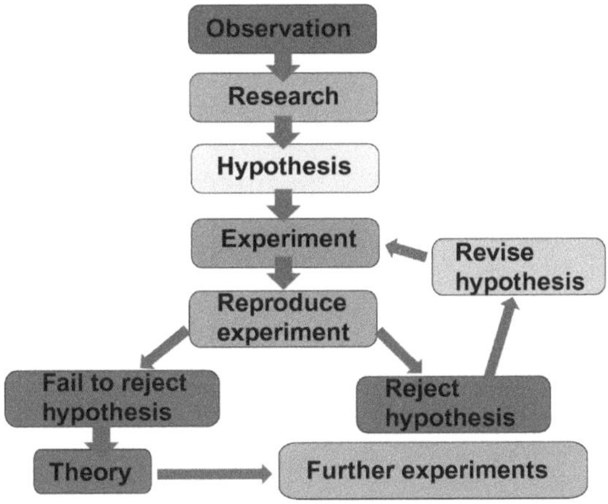

Figure 1.1 Schematic diagram of the scientific method.

theory may be formulated that will be subjected to multiple additional experiments. This approach is in line with the Popper view on science and falsification (Popper, 1963), which is most applicable to the forensic sciences.

OUTLINE OF THE VOLUME

This book is meant to be a brief introduction to professionalism, ethics, and their relevance to the practice of forensic anthropology. As such, we discuss: the need for professional ethics (Chapter 2: The Need for Professional Ethics); currently available ethical guidelines and their means of enforcement (Chapter 3: Current Ethical Guidelines and a Theory of Ethics); the role of the forensic anthropologist in death investigations (Chapter 4: Defining the Role of the Forensic Anthropologist); the use of human remains and human subjects within the context of forensic anthropology (Chapter 5: The use of Human Subjects in Forensic Anthropology Research); analysis, reporting, and testifying (Chapter 6: Reporting and Testifying in Forensic Anthropology); and harassment and discrimination (Chapter 7: Discrimination and Harassment in Forensic Anthropology); with a short summary and concluding remarks (Chapter 8: Looking Backward and Thinking Forward). Finally, as reference material, we have also included a number of appendices.

Forensic anthropology is still a young discipline, just beginning to develop its own standards, define itself as a profession, and to develop best practices. As previously highlighted, it is our hope that the information presented here will serve as a reference for ongoing discussions about the future of the discipline. As forensic anthropology grows and moves forward it will be critical to have a clear outline of professional and ethical practice and behavior, as it is these characteristics that give a discipline authority and support expertise.

CHAPTER 2

The Need for Professional Ethics

The need for professional ethics is rather simple; as Appelbaum (1997:233) suggests, without ethics, a discipline "must tolerate all behaviors equally, since no neutral principle exists for accepting some and condemning others. There can be no good practices and no bad practices." Creating an ethical code for a profession must begin with a group of individuals, typically those on the board of, or tasked by the board of, an organization, choosing which values to the organization and society in general, are most important to promote and uphold (Appelbaum, 1997:235). Additionally, those in charge of creating a code of ethics must justify why some practices should be considered ethical and others unethical; they must also rationalize the theory behind their ethical code. Forensic anthropology exists as a specialized discipline within anthropology, but occurs at the crossroads of medicine, forensic science, and anthropology. As such, forensic anthropologists must consider issues relevant to each of these fields in the practice of their profession.

Within the context of anthropology, as early as 1998, the American Anthropological Association (AAA) made the decision to promote education and the discussion of ethics in anthropology in order to reduce the need for investigation and adjudication of unethical practices (Fluehr-Lobban, 2003:23). While more recently within the context of forensic pathology, Denton (2013:313–314) examined the need for ethical training for forensic pathologists and found the main issues to be:

> *informed consent for obtaining tissue for research, professionalism issues (conflicts of interest, honesty, recognizing medical errors), confidentiality, billing and coding for procedures, and other issues related to transfusions, infected tissues, human experimentation, and autopsies. Ethical issues identified in forensic pathology include quality assurance and disclosure of errors, fatigue and burnout of colleagues, performing a private autopsy after declining jurisdiction for the office, truthful testimony, and remaining an impartial unbiased physician.*

Ethics and Professionalism in Forensic Anthropology. DOI: https://doi.org/10.1016/B978-0-12-812065-1.00002-6

Forensic pathology is not alone in its need for training in ethics, nor in its ethical concerns, as these too are shared by forensic anthropology to varying degrees.

The goal of this chapter is to discuss the need for professional ethics within forensic anthropology in order to maintain scientific integrity and avoid professional misconduct. Because forensic anthropology is a scientific discipline, we must discuss the importance of ethics within a scientific context. Also discussed is the role of the 2009 report by the National Academy of Sciences (NAS) in codifying the need for ethical codes in the forensic sciences, as well as the more recent report authored by the President's Council of Advisors on Science and Technology (PCAST).

SCIENTIFIC INTEGRITY: TRANSPARENCY, MISCONDUCT, AND CONFLICTS OF INTEREST

Scientific integrity has been described as the "commitment to truthfulness, to personal accountability, and to vigorous adherence to standards of professional conduct" (Warner and Weiss, 2004:381). The basis of scientific integrity is the impartial, transparent nature of the scientific process, as well as the public's confidence in the scientific enterprise (Krimsky, 2010:104). Critical to maintaining scientific integrity is the avoidance of misconduct and conflicts of interest (i.e., unethical behavior), which would have a direct impact on scientific reporting and results.

Transparency

Transparency, within the context of science and scientific procedures, is operating in such a way that outside stakeholders can follow any actions performed during scientific/laboratory operations or specific case analyses. Transparency allows for errors (i.e., mistakes), or misconduct, in a case to be tracked and identified, therefore, minimizing the ramifications of such actions and ensuring the quality of the laboratory functions. Scientific integrity and transparency are linked, in that scientific integrity is required for the practice of good science and transparency is the backbone of ensuring and promoting scientific integrity.

The concept of scientific integrity is not new to forensic anthropology. Forensic anthropologists have been practicing and advocating for good scientific practices since the formal inception of the discipline in the 1970s; much of this can be inferred from the legal nature of forensic anthropology and the requirements of truthfulness and accountability while testifying. Transparency, however, is a relatively new concept to the discipline. Only within the last 15 years or so have practices that ensure transparency, such as the use of analytical notes, performance checking of equipment, or laboratory proficiency testing, become more widespread. To become an accredited forensic anthropology laboratory (see Chapter 4: Defining the Role of the Forensic Anthropologist, for further discussion) many of the practices that ensure transparency need to be formalized and practiced routinely. Currently, there are only two accredited forensic anthropology-specific laboratories in the United States: The Central Identification Laboratory (CIL) as part of the Defense POW/MIA Accounting Agency (DPAA) and the forensic anthropology lab within the Harris County Institute of Forensic Sciences (HCIFS). There are a few forensic anthropologists who work full-time in Medical Examiner's Offices that are accredited by the National Association of Medical Examiner's (NAME), as well as the accredited Federal Bureau of Investigation (FBI) Laboratory, but these are not laboratories solely dedicated to forensic anthropological analysis. We argue that the lack of transparency by many practicing forensic anthropologists is not an indication of poor scientific integrity, rather it is related to a disconnect between forensic anthropology laboratory practices and general forensic science practices. With the majority of forensic anthropologists operating from university-based laboratories, they are not exposed to professional laboratory management practices or the importance of documentation from a forensic science laboratory standpoint (which do not typically employ forensic anthropologists). This disconnect often results in a lack of paperwork and documentation, which are meant to aid in creating transparency within the scientific process.

Misconduct

"Professional misconduct" is behavior that is contrary to a professional code of ethics (see Chapter 3: Current Ethical Guidelines and a Theory of Ethics, for codes in forensic anthropology). Misconduct can include sexual harassment, plagiarism, or misrepresenting one's qualifications. The penalties for misconduct are also typically established in a discipline's professional code of ethics, and can range from warnings, to the loss of organizational membership or certification. Of course, if the misconduct involves criminal activity, the individual can suffer legal recourse; however, most unethical behaviors are lawful. This is partially the reason misconduct by government officials is often referred to as "soft corruption" (Sun, 2016), it is insidious and difficult to combat because it is not illegal.

Part of the push to improve the overall state of the forensic sciences, is to develop a research culture in order to promote advancement of the disciplines (Mnookin et al., 2011). To this extent, it is important to also define "research misconduct." The Office of Research Integrity (ORI), as part of the U.S. Department of Health and Human Services (DHHS), has a clear definition of research misconduct, as the "fabrication, falsification, or plagiarism in proposing, performing, or reviewing research, or in reporting research results"[1] Within the forensic sciences, this definition of misconduct could extend not only to research conducted to improve methods, but also to case reports that apply these methods. In terms of forensic anthropology, it is important not to misrepresent oneself or one's qualifications. Additionally, one must not misrepresent or falsify research or the results of analyses; all of which can be considered misconduct. Repercussions for professional and/or research misconduct are discussed further in Chapter 3, Current Ethical Guidelines and a Theory of Ethics.

Conflicts of Interest

Conflicts of interest are violations of practitioner independence and are considered a type of professional misconduct. A Classic example of a conflict of interest is tailoring analytical results to support the interests of the agency funding the analyses. Within forensic anthropology, conflicts of interest may result from poor performance metrics, or a compulsion to please or appease consumers. Koppl (2005) notes that this "motivation bias" (also referred to as "pro-police bias" in Cooley, 2004) can occur if there is too great a dependence on consumer satisfaction, which in turn can create a bias toward pleasing consumers (e.g., police agencies, prosecutors, defense attorneys, supervisors, etc.) in order to stay funded. Motivation bias can also arise from issues relating to personal performance evaluations and future career opportunities. Additionally, a recent study found that forensic scientists (in this case, forensic psychologists and psychiatrists) tended to bias their findings toward the side of the legal team that retained their services;

[1]https://ori.hhs.gov/definition-misconduct

showing evidence for what the authors describe as an "allegiance effect" (Murrie et al., 2013).

Krimsky (2006:62) argues that there are three principals that must exist in order to promote good science (i.e., maintain scientific integrity) in society and avoid conflicts of interest: (1) scientists must be able to conduct research without unjustified restrictions by other authorities (e.g., sponsors, governments, etc.); (2) scientists must be able to report results on their own schedule (i.e., when the analyses are complete, when withholding results could cause harm); and, (3) that parties with vested interests must not be involved with the scientific process, and any attempts to disrupt the scientific process must be held accountable. Within the context of forensic anthropology, avoiding conflicts of interest can be accomplished in part via laboratory accreditation (with routine audits, etc.), and completion of conflict of interest forms, both of which are examples of procedures used to increase and support operational transparency.

Regarding forensic pathology, some investigations into conflicts of interest have been pursued. Using data found in Luzi et al. (2013), Melinek et al. (2013) discuss that over 70% of survey respondents (a total of 336 NAME members) had been pressured to alter their analytical findings, and ~25% had suffered negative consequences for resisting these pressures. Further, some forensic pathologists indicated that their diagnostic decision making was affected through threat of litigation. Perhaps most alarming is that "approximately 10% of respondents had been asked to sign documents (autopsy reports and/or death certificates) that were not consistent with the findings at autopsy" (Melinek et al., 2013:94). Additionally, Melinek et al. (2013) found that many forensic pathologists, when acting as a witness for the prosecution, were expected not to cooperate with the defense, and over half of government employed forensic pathologists had restrictions on their ability to consult privately (likely in regard to concerns about potential conflicts of interest).

Based on these conflicts of interest, Melinek et al. (2013) provide position statements from the NAME Ad Hoc Committee on Medical Examiner Independence. To briefly summarize these statements, their position is: forensic pathologists need to work independently from law enforcement and family pressures; coroner's and medical examiner's offices need to have an open door policy for their experts to consult with any attorneys; no one should be intimidated based on testimony from their scientific conclusions; restrictions on private consultation undermine transparency and scientific integrity; expert testimony should be the same regardless of who has requested the testimony (e.g., prosecution/defense); review of a forensic pathologist/medical examiner/coroner's work should go through a quality assurance process; draft reports should not be made available to outside entities prior to finalization of the report; in regard to analytical conclusions and testimony, the forensic pathologists' opinion is formed independently from the prosecution, even though they may have been working directly with law enforcement or the prosecuting attorneys.

THE NATIONAL ACADEMY OF SCIENCES REPORT

The NAS formed a committee of subject matter experts and forensic science stakeholders to review, survey, and examine the current state and practices of the forensic sciences within the United States; the result of this work was the 2009 NAS Report entitled: *Strengthening Forensic Science in the United States: A Path Forward* (National Research Council, 2009). The impetus for this report was a number of scandals in the forensic sciences, as well as the relatively successful courtroom litigation of a number of testimonies relating to fingerprint and toolmark analyses (Kaye, 2010:8). The 2009 NAS Report found that (1) many practices of forensic scientists were not tested or statistically validated; (2) many forensic scientists could not adequately explain their methods or the statistics involved in how they were able to reach various conclusions, such as how a fingerprint is actually individuated; (3) many forensic labs are underfunded with large backlogs of evidence needing to be processed; and (4) many practices, such as having a forensic laboratory funded by a prosecutor's office, inherently generate the potential for conflicts of interest.

Unlike many disciplines and topics (e.g., forensic odontology and bitemark analysis), forensic anthropology only has two page references listed in the NAS Report's index, and neither directly refer to any negative issues nor calls for reform. Because forensic anthropology was not found to exemplify any issues warranting reform, the primary implications from the NAS Report for forensic anthropology are broad and generalized throughout the forensic sciences as represented in the report's 13 recommendations (see National Research Council, 2009:19–33), which are:

1. "Create a National Institute of Forensic Sciences (NIFS).
2. Standardize terminology and reporting practices.
3. Expand research on the accuracy, reliability, and validity of the forensic sciences.
4. Remove forensic science services from the administrative control of law enforcement agencies and prosecutors' offices.
5. Support forensic science research on human observer bias and sources of error.
6. Develop tools for advancing measurement, validation, reliability, information sharing, and proficiency testing and to establish protocols for examinations, methods, and practices.
7. Require the mandatory accreditation of all forensic laboratories and certification for all forensic science practitioners.
8. Laboratories should establish routine quality assurance procedures.
9. Establish a national code of ethics with a mechanism for enforcement.
10. Support higher education in the form of forensic science graduate programs, to include scholarships and fellowships.
11. Improve the medico–legal death investigation system.
12. Support Automated Fingerprint Information Systems (AFIS) interoperability through the development of standards.
13. Support the use of forensic science in homeland security."

Many of these recommendations are direct attempts to increase scientific integrity and decrease potential avenues for conflicts of interest. Based on these recommendations, the NAS Report's implications for forensic anthropology are that forensic anthropologists must standardize their terminology and reporting practices; expand efforts examining method accuracy, reliability, and validity; examine intra- and interobserver error; develop, perform, and maintain performance checking of equipment and laboratory proficiency testing of analysts; require forensic anthropology laboratory accreditation and individual certification; develop and support laboratory quality assurance procedures (likely required for accreditation); and establish a national ethical code with enforcement.

A number of these recommendations are outside of the scope of this volume; however, we will touch on: ethical code development and enforcement (Chapter 3: Current Ethical Guidelines and a Theory of Ethics), performance checking and proficiency testing, accreditation and certification (Chapter 4: Defining the Role of the Forensic Anthropologist), and reporting (Chapter 6: Reporting and Testifying in Forensic Anthropology).

PRESIDENT'S COUNCIL OF ADVISORS ON SCIENCE AND TECHNOLOGY REPORT ON FORENSIC SCIENCE IN CRIMINAL COURTS

In 2016 the PCAST released a report to the President of the United States entitled: *Forensic Science in Criminal Courts: Ensuring Scientific Validity of Feature-Comparison Methods*. This work was a response to the highly critical NAS report that highlighted deficiencies in the science introduced as part of forensic analyses. The goal of this report was to identify additional steps necessary to ensure the scientific validity of such analyses presented in court. This report is primarily concerned with addressing scientific validity of various feature-comparison methods, which include analyses of: DNA, bitemarks, fingerprints, hair, footprints, and firearms. Various recommendations are given for the National Institute of Standards and Technology (NIST) and the Organization of Scientific Area Committees (OSAC; discussed further in Chapter 4: Defining the Role of the Forensic Anthropologist), as well as the FBI, the Attorney General, and the judiciary. Anthropology is not mentioned explicitly in the report (President's Committee of Advisors on Science and Technology Panel on Educational Technology, 2016). However, there is one area where forensic anthropology may need to incorporate the findings in this report: toolmark analysis. Analyses in this area should ensure that they follow the guidelines for "foundational validity" as outlined in the report. The method must be "reproducible and consistent," and should provide "empirical estimates" to include false positive rates and sensitivity (President's Committee of Advisors on Science and Technology Panel on Educational Technology, 2016:146).

THE NEED FOR TRAINING AND EDUCATION IN ETHICS

Recently, Denton (2013:312) suggested the addition of an "ethical issues in forensic pathology" educational module to the core training of forensic pathologists; stating "the practice of forensic pathology is unique and has its own special ethical issues, requiring active intentional education". Denton suggests that incorporating both lecture and case-based education has been successful in surgical residency programs, and thus would also benefit forensic pathology. Further, Denton (2013) surveyed forensic pathology fellowship directors and found that most (24 of 27; 89%) do not have a formal forensic pathology ethics lecture as part of their programs, but that 85% (23 of 27) thought it would be worthwhile for them or NAME to develop an educational module on ethics in forensic pathology.

Forensic anthropology is in a similar situation. Most, if not all, academic programs that provide training in forensic anthropology lack education on ethics outside of bioarchaeological issues such as those related to the Native American Graves Protection and Repatriation Act (NAGPRA) and cultural patrimony. However, the need for training in ethics for forensic anthropology is paramount. Much of our standard operating procedures (SOPs) for field and laboratory work were developed to generate transparency and maintain scientific integrity to avoid conflicts of interest and promote "good science." Further, as professionals we are often required to complete forms regarding conflicts of interest, take part in Institutional Review Boards (IRB; discussed further in Chapter 5: The use of Human Subjects in Forensic Anthropology Research), and to act in an ethical manner as required by our membership to various professional affiliations. We must consider ethics an important part of our professional careers; thus, we must also consider training our students and mentees in the importance of ethical behavior. Further, professionals tasked with educating students on ethics must stay up-to-date with changes in relevant legislation and policies. It is therefore essential for professionals to have venues to discuss these topics in places such as peer-reviewed journals or workshops at professional meetings and to provide funding for such efforts.

CONCLUSIONS

Scientific integrity and transparency are essential to the practice of all professional science. Identifying and avoiding misconduct and conflicts of interest are key to maintaining scientific integrity. Professional ethics, such as the ethical codes (discussed in Chapter 3: Current Ethical Guidelines and a Theory of Ethics), exist to provide guidelines for professional behavior, including the promotion of scientific integrity and the identification and reporting of professional misconduct. The NAS report highlighted various deficiencies within the forensic sciences, several of which can be remedied with stronger ethical codes and guidelines. The remainder of this book will explore these issues as relevant to forensic anthropology.

CHAPTER 3

Current Ethical Guidelines and a Theory of Ethics

The previous chapter discussed the necessity for a code of ethics within the forensic sciences, specifically within forensic anthropology. Here we seek to expand on this need and explore the current state of ethics within the discipline. Our goals for this chapter are to discuss: (1) the primary ethical codes for forensic anthropology, including their enforcement; (2) the theory of ethics in relation to forensic anthropology; (3) how other more general ethical approaches relate, or apply, to forensic anthropology; and (4) offer expansions of the current ethical codes applicable to forensic anthropologists.

ETHICS IN FORENSIC SCIENCE

In response to the NAS report (National Research Council, 2009) the National Commission on Forensic Science (NCFS), a federal advisory committee developed by NIST and the United States Department of Justice (DOJ), recently published the National Code of Ethics and Professional Responsibility for the Forensic Sciences (NCEPRFS). This Code has 16 requirements that center on proper conduct regarding analyses and reporting as well as representation and working within one's own area of expertise. The code also highlights the need for continuing education, certification, proficiency testing, and to publish and present research results. The NCFS recommends that "the US Attorney General should direct the forensic science and forensic medicine service providers within the DOJ to adopt the National Code of Ethics and Professional Responsibility for Forensic Science and Forensic Medicine Service Providers, that the Code be annually reviewed and signed by all forensic science and forensic medicine service providers, and that steps be defined to enforce violations."[1]

[1]https://www.justice.gov/archives/ncfs/page/file/788576/download

Ethics and Professionalism in Forensic Anthropology. DOI: https://doi.org/10.1016/B978-0-12-812065-1.00003-8

The NCEPRFS is meant to only apply to service providers within the DOJ, and there are no proposed means of enforcement. Further, in its current form, this code is simply a recommendation to the US Attorney General, with no indications that it will be considered, adopted, or implemented. Nevertheless, this code represents a major step forward in acknowledging the lack of ethical codes for forensic science practitioners as well as the need for oversight of such codes. Moreover, the content of this code is well constructed and touches on most of the important aspects needed in ethical codes.

CURRENT PROFESSIONAL ORGANIZATIONS AND CODES OF ETHICS FOR FORENSIC ANTHROPOLOGISTS

The Scientific Working Group for forensic anthropology (SWGAnth) is based in the United States and was established by the Joint POW/MIA Accounting Agency—Central Identification Laboratory (JPAC-CIL, now the Scientific Analysis Directorate of the DPAA) and the FBI (Langley and Tersigni-Tarrant, 2017). Because of the creation of the OSAC by the NIST (see Chapter 4: Defining the Role of the Forensic Anthropologist), the group is currently on an indefinite hiatus; however, prior to this break, it generated a number of best practice guidelines, including one for ethical behavior in forensic anthropology (Appendix B.1; SWGAnth, 2013a). Unlike the ethical codes associated with professional organizations, the SWGAnth best practice guidelines have no membership requirements or official means of regulation or enforcement. Rather, these best practice documents are meant to serve as consensus guidelines for forensic anthropologists with the caveat that if an individual does not follow best practice procedures, they may have to explain why they deviated from these guidelines during testimony.

As briefly mentioned in Chapter 1, Introduction to Professionalism, Ethics, and Forensic Anthropology, there are already various ethical codes to which forensic anthropologists may be beholden, most of which are associated with professional organizations. The majority of individuals practicing forensic anthropology within the United States are members of the Anthropology Section of the AAFS. To a lesser extent, forensic anthropologists in the United States may also hold professional membership in the ABFA (requiring certification by the ABFA), the Society of Forensic Anthropologists (SOFA), or the

AAPA. Additionally, while not the primary affiliations for forensic anthropologists in the United States, the National Association for the Practice of Anthropology (NAPA), a section of the AAA, is primarily devoted to the professionalization and ethical considerations of anthropologists working outside of academia; and the Society for American Archaeology (SAA) has many American forensic archaeologist members due to membership restrictions in the Anthropology Section of the AAFS[2].

Outside of the United States, professional associations appropriate for forensic anthropology (and/or forensic archaeology) are limited. There is the Forensic Anthropology Society of Europe (FASE), which is a subsection of the International Academy of Legal Medicine (IALM). The FASE has no published ethical code; however, they do state that one of their aims is to "encourage and promote adherence to high standards of ethics, conduct and professional practice in forensic anthropology"[3]. The Latin American Forensic Anthropology Association or Asociación Latinoamericana de Antropología Forense (ALAF) also does not have a published set of ethical standards that apply to its members; however, they too claim as part of their goals "to establish ethical and professional criteria for the practice of Forensic Anthropology"[4]. The British Association for Forensic Anthropology (BAFA), established under the umbrella of the British Association for Human Identification (BAHI), has a lengthy "Code of Practice, Ethics and Professional Standards" developed in conjunction with the Royal Anthropological Institute of Great Britain and Ireland and the Forensic Regulator in the United Kingdom (UK). The Chartered Institute for Archaeologists (CIfA), which is a professional organization for forensic archaeologists practicing in the United Kingdom has both a code of conduct and regulations for professional conduct. A bit further afield is the British Association for Biological Anthropology and Osteoarchaeology (BABAO), a United Kingdom-based organization with primary interest in bioarchaeology, but extends to all disciplines of biological anthropology (to include forensic anthropology), that has a published code of ethics.

[2]In 2014 the section changed its name from Physical Anthropology to Anthropology in order to allow for a broader definition and membership of individuals practicing forensic anthropology, primarily forensic archaeologists.
[3]http://www.forensicanthropology.eu/index.php/about
[4]http://en.alafforense.org/index.html

While each organization's ethical code shares similar principles, they also differ to varying degrees. The ethical codes of these organizations, both within and outside of the United States, are discussed later. Each code's web address is presented in Appendix C, Websites of Ethical Codes (accessed November 2017).

American Academy of Forensic Sciences

The "Code of Ethics and Conduct" published by the AAFS is succinct in its coverage of four main principles. The first principle deals with conduct in line with the "best interests and objectives of the Academy."[5] The second two principles relate to misrepresentation; members or affiliates should not misrepresent themselves (e.g., in education, training, membership status, experience) or their data and final professional opinion. The final section of the code prohibits members or affiliates from issuing public statements that might appear to reflect the official opinions of the Academy without prior approval from the Board of Directors.

American Board of Forensic Anthropology

The code of ethics espoused by the ABFA is also rather brief. They include the four principles as in the AAFS code, but further expand theirs to include four additional principles. These are: (1) to make statements that are technically sound and based in science; (2) be impartial, unbiased, logical, clear, and concise; (3) not to work on a contingency fee basis and to charge reasonable fees for services; and (4) keep information confidential. The ABFA also requires current Diplomates to signatorially endorse this Code of Ethics annually. While the ABFA is primarily concerned with overseeing the certification of forensic anthropologists within the United States, their policies and procedures manual states that one of their missions is "[t]o encourage and promote adherence to high standards of ethics, conduct, and professional practice in forensic anthropology"[6].

American Association of Physical Anthropologists

The AAPA's "Code of Ethics" for biological anthropologists is broken down into three major areas: research, teaching, and application. From their ethical code: "The purpose of this Code is to provide

[5]https://www.aafs.org/aafs-ethics/
[6]Published theabfa.org

AAPA members and other interested persons with guidelines for making ethical choices in the conduct of their physical anthropological work"[7]. The research section covers issues ranging from responsibly interacting with research subjects; responsibility to scholarship and science; responsibility to the public, including informed consent, respect, and treatment of research subjects; data usage and access; and dissemination and accessibility of research and results. The teaching section covers responsibility to students and trainees, including professional conduct, mentorship, and dedication to instruction. The application section covers responsibilities regarding the practice of biological anthropology, including professional conduct, collegiality, and leadership.

Society of Forensic Anthropologists

The "Guidelines for Professional Conduct" of the SOFA has nine main points. There is overlap with the ABFA and the AAFS, e.g., not to misrepresent oneself or data, to keep materials confidential, and to be grounded in science. Where the SOFA code differs, is that it does not require behavior that is in the best interest of the organization, although it does include a requirement of collegiality, and that "motives, methods, and actions shall at all times be above reproach and conducted with respect for human dignity"[8]. While this last statement is rather broad, it does attempt to expand the scope of ethics within the field and move toward a theory of ethics (discussed later).

Scientific Working Group—Forensic Anthropology

The SWGAnth has created a comprehensive "Code of Ethics and Conduct" that states, "Forensic Anthropologists shall not misrepresent themselves or their work, misappropriate tangible or intellectual property, evade the truth, conspire to deceive, demonstrate disrespect to the dead or their family members, or otherwise betray the confidence placed in them by the public" (see Appendix B.1; SWGAnth, 2013a). The code then elaborates on this statement by providing 21 guidelines for appropriate behavior. This code expands on that of the AAFS, ABFA, and SOFA to include statements on data collection, intellectual independence, reporting ethics violations, disclosure of conflicts of interest, and respect for the decedent and the family.

[7]http://physanth.org/about/committees/ethics/aapa-code-ethics-and-other-ethics-resources/
[8]http://www.sofainc.org/code-of-ethics

American Anthropological Association

The AAA, an organization that covers all primary subfields of anthropology (i.e., archaeology, biological anthropology, linguistic anthropology, and sociocultural anthropology), has an ethics statement available in the AAA Ethics Blog.[9] The original Principles of Professional Responsibility were written by a special Committee on Ethics of the AAA and published in 1971 (Fluehr-Lobban, 2003). The seven principles of the AAA ethics code are: (1) do no harm, (2) be open and honest regarding your work, (3) obtain informed consent and necessary permissions, (4) weigh competing ethical obligations, (5) make results accessible, (6) protect and preserve records, and (7) maintain respectful and ethical professional relationships.[10] The importance of this document, as described by Fluehr-Lobban (2003:227) is that it argues: "[i]n research, anthropologists' paramount responsibility is to those they study. When there is a conflict of interest, these individuals must come first." Expanding this to forensic anthropology, we can argue that individuals (representing casework or research) must come before the interests of the forensic anthropologist (see also Chapter 5: The use of Human Subjects in Forensic Anthropology Research).

National Association for the Practice of Anthropology

From an applied (primarily sociocultural) anthropological perspective, the NAPA (a section of the AAA) provides six ethical guidelines: (1) respect for human rights and welfare of individuals affected by anthropological research and practice; (2) timely disclosure of objectives, methods and sponsorship of research activities to research subjects; (3) professional conduct and timely communication of findings and recommendations to invested parties (often employers); (4) a commitment to professional interactions and mentorship with students and trainees; (5) a responsibility to perform work in a manner that supports and encourages other professional work; and (6) a responsibility to the discipline of anthropology to promote the field in a favorable manner.[11]

Society for American Archaeology

The SAA provides archaeological ethics based on eight principles: (1) *Stewardship* of remains, artifacts, and depositional data; (2)

[9] http://ethics.americananthro.org/category/statement/
[10] http://ethics.americananthro.org/category/statement/
[11] http://practicinganthropology.org/about/ethical-guidelines/

Accountability for developing working relationships with affected parties regarding research and excavation; (3) *Commercialization* or the discouragement of turning archaeological materials or sites into commodities; (4) *Public education and outreach* with interested parties to encourage the preservation, protection, and interpretation of the archaeological record; (5) *Intellectual property* or treating the documents and research generated from the archaeological record as valuable materials which should be made available to interested parties; (6) *Public reporting and publication* or making the results of archaeological investigations accessible within a reasonable time; (7) *Records and preservation* or the need for archaeologists to actively preserve and make accessible collections, records, and reports; and (8) *Training and resources* or the fact that individuals must only pursue work that is consistent with their training, experience, facilities, and other support as needed.

British Association for Forensic Anthropology

The BAFA has a published "Code of Practice, Ethics and Professional Standards in Forensic Anthropology." This document is quite long and is primarily focused on establishing SOPs for forensic anthropological recoveries and analyses, as well as the role of the expert witness. "A Theory of Ethics" section outlines "ethics and conduct" in which it is stated that "[f]orensic anthropologists shall not misrepresent themselves or their work, misappropriate tangible or intellectual property, evade the truth, conspire to deceive, demonstrate disrespect to the dead or their family members, or otherwise betray the confidence placed in them by the public"[12]. The code goes on to outline 25 actions requisite for ethical behavior within the discipline. Much of what is in the code of ethics of the SWGAnth is also in this code; however, the BAFA also includes guidelines for the use of case photos and data, taking action on ethics violations when in a supervisory role, and sensitivities in terms of cultural and religious views of human remains. The final point (#25) deals with sanctions, in that misconduct will be handled with the professional body and/or the employer. Additionally, the Forensic Science Regulator may be involved in addressing misconduct.

[12]https://www.therai.org.uk/images/stories/Forensic/Code%20of%20Practice%20Ethics%20and%20Professional%20Standards%20in%20Forensic%20Anthropology-Draft.pdf

Chartered Institute for Archaeologists

The eight principles of the SAA are echoed in the five principles of the Code of Conduct of the CIfA. However, the CIfA also includes a principle regarding professionalism and collegiality (Principle 5), which states: "The archaeologist shall recognize the aspirations of employees, colleagues, and helpers with regard to all matters relating to employment, including career development, health and safety, terms and conditions of employment, and equality of opportunity."[13]

British Association for Biological Anthropology and Osteoarchaeology

The ethics statement of the BABAO is quite long and, much like the AAPA, is focused on research, teaching, and application, as well as dissemination of results. This code is generally applicable to forensic anthropology in terms of establishing scientific integrity and transparency in data collection and reporting. However, it does not address all the ethical situations encountered in the profession of forensic anthropology, to include expert testimony, ensuring adequate training and expertise to perform forensic analyses, the need to keep materials confidential, and maintaining impartiality.

Applying the ethical principles of anthropology, archaeology, and biological anthropology to forensic anthropology includes principles ranging from do no harm and respect for human rights; to issues regarding commercialization and intellectual property; to education and training; collegiality; mentorship; and access to research, research materials, and data. Much of these more detail-oriented ethical principles are absent from even the SWGAnth Ethics Guidelines; however, they must be considered when developing a theory of ethics for forensic anthropology (discussed further in the later sections).

MEANS OF LODGING A COMPLAINT AND ENFORCEMENT OF ETHICAL VIOLATIONS

The three primary ethical codes for forensic anthropology, at least within the United States, are those of the AAFS, the ABFA, and the AAPA. Here we are excluding the SWGAnth Ethics Guideline because, as previously stated, despite being the most robust ethical code available to forensic anthropologists, it has no organizational

[13]http://www.concernedhistorians.org/content_files/file/et/70.pdf, page 1

affiliation nor means of enforcement. While each professional organization may differ on the reporting practices for alleging misconduct and enforcement, there are similar themes that may be found in various ethical codes, which are highlighted here.

American Academy of Forensic Sciences

Lodging a Complaint. According to the AAFS Policy and Procedure Manual,[14] the Ethics Committee may initiate an investigation into ethics violations if: (1) the Academy Executive Director receives from a member or affiliate a written complaint alleging ethics violations of another member or affiliate, or (2) a motion is made by any member of the Ethics Committee based on evidence of an ethical violation by a member or affiliate. Investigations will only be made on ethics violations occurring within the previous 5 years. Within 30 days of receiving a complaint the Ethics Committee must determine if the complaint is within their purview and there is probable cause for a violation. If a claim is under the jurisdiction of the Ethics Committee and there is probable cause, the accused is notified of the complaint. The accused has 30 days to respond to the allegation. After a response is received the Ethics Committee will determine if a formal hearing is warranted. The Ethics Committee oversees the hearing as outlined in the AAFS Policy and Procedure Manual. At the termination of the hearing the Ethics Committee submits their findings to the Board of Directors, who will determine the appropriate level of sanction.

Enforcement of Ethics Violations. The Board of Directors of the AAFS will decide the appropriate sanction based on the nature of the violation. If the violation is considered minor the member or affiliate may receive either a confidential "Letter of Reprimand" or nonconfidential "Letter of Censure." If the violation is serious, membership or affiliation with the AAFS can be suspended. If the violation is egregious, membership may be revoked. To aid in determining the nature of the violation the Board of Directors considers various questions: is the behavior part of a pattern?, was it intentional?, did the accused express remorse?, are there previous sanctions of the accused?, among others.

[14]Published online at https://www.aafs.org/wp-content/uploads/MASTER-PPM.pdf

American Board of Forensic Anthropology

Lodging a Complaint. The Ethics Committee may initiate an investigation based on any evidence that necessitates further inquiry. If the initial investigation yields evidence that a complaint is founded, the Ethics Committee will formally hear the charges. At the conclusion of the hearing the Ethics Committee will provide findings and recommendations to the ABFA Board of Directors.

Enforcement of Ethics Violations. The ABFA Board of Directors will consider the recommendations for sanction and upon a three-fourths vote. The accused may be reprimanded, suspended, or decertified.

American Association of Physical Anthropologists

Lodging a Complaint. The AAPA has an ethics committee, but it is a nonadjudicative body. Instead, the committee offers "Ethics Consultations" to current members who may like assistance with an ethical concern or question.

Enforcement of Ethics Violations. Currently, the AAPA has no process for adjudication of claims of unethical behavior and accordingly does not provide sanctions to members for ethical violations.

A THEORY OF ETHICS

A theory of ethics for a discipline is the justification for a set of principles that constitutes the ethical framework of that discipline (Appelbaum, 1997, 2008). In terms of forensic anthropology, if we consider the justification for the current ethical codes to which the majority of forensic anthropologists are beholden, it would appear that while concepts such as the misrepresentation of credentials/expertise and avoiding bias in casework are present, significant portions of these ethical codes are dedicated to the preservation of the organization to which the codes are associated. That is not to say that these organizations should not be concerned with the conduct of their members, but rather, organizational ethical codes are often not "practice-friendly," with ethical codes primarily referring to general conduct (Briody and Pester, 2014). As Pellegrino (2002:383–384) notes, regardless of discipline, many of today's professional societies are primarily concerned with financial survival, corporate growth, investment strategies, and benefits for members, rather than fostering ethical socialization and professional development opportunities.

The current AAFS and ABFA ethical codes are examples of such organizational strategies; both codes lack ethical theory beyond their primary concern that their members do not misrepresent the professional organizations or themselves. While there is nothing wrong with this approach, such ethical codes do little to serve their professional communities. The SWGAnth Ethics Guideline is much more appropriate in regard to the practice of forensic anthropology; dealing with issues ranging from respect for the deceased, scientific integrity, and personal conduct. However, unlike the organizational ethics codes, the SWGAnth Ethics Guideline lacks procedures for reporting violations or enacting sanctions. Further, even the SWGAnth Ethics Guideline, while being the most applicable ethical code, does not present a clear ethical theory, nor does it discuss the ethics of science or the relational nature of forensic anthropology to medicine or more directly the discipline of forensic pathology.

Ethics of Science

Stepping back from anthropology and medicine, forensic anthropology is, of course, one of the forensic sciences requiring the application of, and adherence to, the scientific method. The ethical practice of science in general has been discussed by various authors, typically within the context of science education, and requires: (1) the proper use of the scientific method, (2) using generally accepted practices within the field, and (3) avoiding scientific misconduct (i.e., acting unethically) (Consoli, 2006).

Applying the ethics of science to forensic anthropology, the ethical principles of proper scientific practices and general acceptance of methods by a discipline are represented in the Daubert standard[15] as part of the admissibility in court, while the issue of avoiding scientific misconduct is represented in the ethical codes of various professional organizations (e.g., the AAFS).

Ethics of Medicine and Forensic Medicine

The ethics of modern medicine are focused on two principles: *beneficence*—to do something to benefit others, and *nonmalfeasance*—to avoid doing harm, if at all possible (Appelbaum, 1997). To put it

[15]The Daubert standard relates to the case of Daubert v. Merrell Dow Pharmaceuticals, Inc. in which standards for the admissibility of an expert witness's testimony were established. The Daubert standard will be discussed further in Chapter 4, Defining the Role of the Forensic Anthropologist.

simply, a medical professional must always do no harm, while also striving to benefit others. However, the difference between clinical medicine and legal medicine is significant; while clinicians promote health, forensic scientists seek justice (Appelbaum, 1997). Thus the applicability of traditional medical ethics to forensic medicine is not straightforward. In fact, Appelbaum (within the context of forensic psychiatry) argues that the principles of *beneficence* and *nonmalfeasance* are rather unimportant in a forensic context because of the lack of a doctor/patient relationship (Appelbaum, 1997:238). While these principles can still apply to forensic medicine, there are two other principles that are more applicable: *truth-telling* and *respect for persons*. Appelbaum's reasoning is that rather than practicing *beneficence* and *nonmalfeasance* for the patient, the forensic doctor must provide relevant information to the court regardless which side of the case the information assists. So, instead of considering *beneficence* and *nonmalfeasance* the backbone of ethical forensic medicine, Appelbaum (1997:239-240) suggests forensic practitioners (in this case, forensic psychiatrists) must value the ethics of *truth-telling:* or "...to tell the truth, the whole truth, and nothing but the truth". In addition to *respect for persons:* maintaining confidentiality and impartiality, while acting to negate potential conflicts of interest associated with one's role in an investigation. Within the context of forensic psychiatry, Appelbaum (1997) suggests this typically includes relying on the concept of informed consent, which of course is not typically possible in many other forensic disciplines, such as forensic pathology or forensic anthropology.

Ethics of Forensic Anthropology

Applying the ethical principle of *nonmalfeasance* to forensic anthropology is a simple and straightforward task. The forensic anthropologist must always do no harm in regard to: damaging/destroying evidence, affecting family members or other parties, the process of the investigation, or any courtroom testimony. However, the applicability of *beneficence* to forensic anthropology is more ambiguous owing to the various consumers of forensic anthropology and forensic science in general (see Chapter 4: Defining the Role of the Forensic Anthropologist). The practice of forensic anthropology results in various benefits to society, such as a deterrence to crime, the resolution of missing persons cases, closure to families, and the determination that remains do not have medicolegal significance, and thus do not need further investigation and resources. Thus, performing an analysis with the intent to benefit a particular party would be a conflict of interest.

The principles of forensic medicine are more applicable to forensic anthropology. *Truth-telling*, and more generally *transparency*, are tenants not only of good science, but routine in the note-taking, reporting, and testimony of the forensic sciences in general. Further, *respect for persons* is also a familiar concept within most forensic sciences, especially forensic anthropology. Unlike many other disciplines, significant portions of anthropological training and coursework are devoted to understanding and respecting human variation—biologically, culturally, linguistically, and temporally.

CONSIDERATIONS FOR EXPANDING ETHICAL CODES IN FORENSIC ANTHROPOLOGY

As one of the forensic sciences, forensic anthropology must adhere to the ethics of science and the medicolegal realm. As a specialization within anthropology, forensic anthropologists are also tied to the ethical codes developed in the greater discipline of anthropology. Further, due to the applied medicolegal nature of forensic anthropological casework, not to mention the historic development of the discipline primarily through medicine and anatomy, forensic anthropology has heavy ties to forensic medicine. We, therefore, argue that a holistic ethical code for forensic anthropology must incorporate aspects from all of these various disciplines, as all are involved in the actual practice of forensic anthropology.

Considering these concepts, we propose a theory of ethics for forensic anthropology must be based on the need for forensic anthropologists to: (1) follow all forensic, legal, medical, and evidentiary requirements (i.e., *truth-telling*); (2) not misrepresent oneself or one's findings (i.e., *truth-telling*); (3) treat remains, casework, colleagues, and invested parties with professional and cultural respect (i.e., *respect for persons*); (4) only perform tasks which they are competent to (i.e., not misrepresent themselves or their qualifications); (5) do no harm (i.e., *nonmalfeasance*); (6) follow the scientific method in a systematic, transparent manner (i.e., *maintain scientific integrity*); (7) document actions in a traceable manner (i.e., *maintain transparency*); (8) avoid and report conflicts of interest and misconduct (i.e., act in an ethical manner); (9) maintain confidentiality of materials (i.e., *respect for persons*); (10) avoid intellectual, personal, financial, and/or emotional biases (i.e., avoid conflicts of interest); (11) manage the use and access of evidence, research facilities, collections, and data in a fair, transparent manner (i.e., *stewardship*); (12) conduct research in a systematic, ethical manner (further discussed in Chapter 5: The use of Human Subjects in Forensic Anthropology Research); and (13) follow all applicable standards and guidelines pertaining to the performance of analyses (i.e., testing), individual qualification, and laboratory accreditation.

At present, the discipline of forensic anthropology has no overarching ethical code that is accepted by all practicing forensic anthropologists (within the United States or abroad). The closest any ethical code comes is the guideline published by the SWGAnth. However, while the SWGAnth Ethics Guideline is longer and more detailed than those of most professional organizations, it is still lacking in various topics and issues. Further, while most organizations have their own ethical codes, one issue with having ethical codes attached to specific organizations is that individuals can simply withdraw from the organization rather than face repercussions for their actions. There is currently no oversight body to track or manage ethical complaints or unethical behavior (Murphy, 2000), which makes these ethical codes unenforceable. As forensic anthropology grows as a discipline it will become even more important to have a code of ethics that contains ethical theory as well as guidelines for behaviors in a single document. Ideally, this code would be enforceable through a formal Ethics Committee within a professional organization that manages some form of certification.

CONCLUSIONS

The currently available ethical codes that are meant to govern the practice of forensic anthropology have various drawbacks and lack a theory of ethics, which is needed to effectively serve the discipline. The current ethical codes that have the potential for enforcement focus on protecting the parent organization, rather than serving their disciplines. We argue that a code of ethics for forensic anthropology must take into consideration scientific, medical, forensic, and anthropological issues in order to be holistic and guide both personal and professional conduct. Further, we argue that this code of ethics needs to be enforceable and overarching regardless of which organization the individual may be a member.

CHAPTER 4

Defining the Role of the Forensic Anthropologist

As we introduced in Chapter 1, Introduction to Professionalism, Ethics, and Forensic Anthropology, forensic anthropology primarily pertains to the recovery and analysis of human skeletal remains in a medicolegal context (Christensen et al., 2014). However, this general definition does not clearly outline exactly what is within the purview of the forensic anthropologist, nor does it define the qualifications required to be a forensic anthropologist. While typical forensic anthropological work is considered to be the recovery and analysis of unidentified human skeletal remains in order to establish identity and contribute to the cause of death, forensic anthropology is a broader discipline. For example, forensic anthropologists can be called in to assist with issues such as repatriation relating to NAGPRA, and identification and age estimation among the living.

The goals of this chapter are to discuss (1) forensic anthropology as a profession; (2) the forensic anthropologist as a subject matter expert within the context of medicolegal death investigation; (3) the differences between qualification, certification, and accreditation within the context of forensic anthropology; and (4) for whom forensic anthropologists work.

PROFESSIONALISM AND THE PROFESSION OF FORENSIC ANTHROPOLOGY

As discussed in previous chapters, a forensic anthropologist is a properly trained subject matter expert, who will analyze a case without a conflict of interest and adheres to an appropriate code of ethics. The types of analyses and conclusions that are appropriate for a forensic anthropologist to conduct or make are relatively well defined. The primary textbooks for forensic anthropology (e.g., Christensen et al.,

Ethics and Professionalism in Forensic Anthropology. DOI: https://doi.org/10.1016/B978-0-12-812065-1.00004-X

2014; Langley and Tersigni-Tarrant, 2017) focus on the following skills: osteology, the determination of medicolegal significance, forensic archaeological methods, the estimation of the biological profile, the analysis of trauma and taphonomy (including the estimation of the postmortem interval via tissue decomposition), and the identification of unknown remains.

However, simply determining the primary subjects in which a forensic anthropologist must be well versed is not enough. A forensic anthropologist is part of a larger profession, and must adhere to professional standards. Following Pellegrino (2002:378) we can define a profession (and by extensions, a professional) as (1) possessing a body of specialized knowledge, (2) practicing within an ethical framework, (3) fulfilling some societal need, and (4) having some form of social mandate allowing for latitude in a discipline's ability to set standards for education and performance of its practitioners.

In fulfillment of the first requirement, forensic anthropologists possess a unique knowledge base of archaeological methods, skeletal biology, cultural context, and analytical reporting skills. While many aspects of this knowledge-base are accessible through general training in biological anthropology and/or archaeology, only individuals further trained in working within the medicolegal system have the requisite forensic anthropological knowledge to *actually practice* forensic anthropology (see below for further discussion). Forensic anthropologists in the United States meet the second requirement of working within an ethical framework by adhering to the ethical codes of relevant professional organizations, primarily the AAFS and/or the ABFA (although, as we argued in Chapter 2: The Need for Professional Ethics and Chapter 3: Current Ethical Guidelines and a Theory of Ethics, there is room for improvement in these ethical codes). The third requirement is met as forensic anthropologists fulfill a societal need by using their unique skillset to assist with the resolution of medicolegal cases. Lastly, Pellegrino's (2002) fourth requirement is currently in the process of being established within forensic anthropology via the NIST OSAC's effort to generate published standards and guidelines for various aspects of forensic anthropological practice. However, this work is far from complete (discussed further in this chapter under "Standards Boards").

Following these criteria, it is critical for a profession to have standards regarding ethical behavior, educational requirements (i.e., Qualifications), licensing (i.e., Certification), and processes for quality assurance and traceability (i.e., Accreditation) to which its practitioners must adhere. In the following sections, we will discuss the latter three issues within the current state of forensic anthropology.

QUALIFICATIONS, CERTIFICATIONS, AND ACCREDITATIONS IN FORENSIC ANTHROPOLOGY

Qualifications

The qualifications for a discipline can be thought of as the professional education or training requirements considered to provide individuals with adequate knowledge to perform discipline-related tasks. The certification of individuals is often considered a qualification; however, here we will consider these as two separate, but related, issues. The current qualifications for forensic anthropology are not well defined. This likely has to do with the relatively young nature of the discipline, the lack of true educational degrees in forensic anthropology, the relative rarity of full-time positions in forensic anthropology, and the current state of certifications in forensic anthropology.

The SWGAnth produced guidelines for both Qualifications (see section "SWGAnth Guideline: Qualifications" in Appendix B; SWGAnth, 2010) and Education and Training (see section "SWGAnth Guideline: Education and Training" Appendix B; SWGAnth, 2013b) for forensic anthropologists. The SWGAnth Qualifications guideline discusses what different individuals are qualified to do based on varying levels of personal qualification, including certification. Within the Qualifications guideline, the SWGAnth recommends three levels of qualification, with "Forensic Anthropologist I" filling the role of a student in forensic anthropology, acting as a laboratory assistant; "Forensic Anthropologist II" being an individual with at least a master's degree that can author and sign reports, preferably under the supervision of a "Forensic Anthropologist III". And a "Forensic Anthropologist III" being an individual with a PhD that is certified in forensic anthropology by an accredited organization (such as the ABFA).

The SWGAnth Education and Training guideline on the other hand, presents: "themes and topics designed to provide students and professionals with the basic knowledge and skills required to both meet qualification guidelines... and practice forensic anthropology" (SWGAnth, 2013b:1). This guideline discusses primary and secondary educational areas in which it recommends university-level coursework, the necessity of training outside the classroom in various techniques and procedures, and various supplemental (continuing) education options. This guideline also discusses the need for practical training outside of the classroom by a verified trainer (in theory, a certified forensic anthropologist), as well as research into relevant areas and continuing education. As part of the recertification process within the ABFA, there is a section on continuing education, which can include attendance at workshops, conferences, lectures, and undertaking independent research. However, continuing education is only one component of the recertification process and can be overlooked in lieu of other evidence of activity in the field (e.g., case reports, court appearances, committee assignments, etc.).

Currently, the SWGAnth guideline for Education and Training in forensic anthropology is essentially a suggestion and there are no standards available to define the education and training required to become a forensic anthropologist. In 2004 the AAFS established a standing committee called the Forensic Science Education Programs Accreditation Commission (FEPAC) to oversee accreditation of academic programs awarding bachelor's or master's degrees in forensic science, or with a forensic science or digital evidence concentration. The FEPAC has a published set of policies and procedures[1] that outline the organization and the process of program accreditation. Within this document, there is an acknowledgment that it may be appropriate to grow the scope of accreditation within the forensic sciences, and they outline a path for other programs and disciplines within the field to develop a set of standards for accreditation. Implementing such standards for programs that grant degrees in forensic anthropology, or developing a similar standard for other programs that specialize in forensic anthropology training, even if the degree is still in anthropology, may be beneficial in the future to demonstrate the requisite academic qualifications and training.

[1] http://fepac-edu.org/sites/default/files/FEPAC%20Policies%20%26%20Procedures%2008032016.pdf

It is not uncommon for forensic practitioners to use an organization's membership status in place of a qualification. As previously discussed, for forensic anthropology in the United States the most applicable organization is the Anthropology Section of the AAFS. Within this organization there are five primary levels of membership: Student Affiliate, Trainee Affiliate, Associate Member, Member, and Fellow. The first three are considered entry-level categories; requirements for the other categories are more extensive. Individual sections within the AAFS determine their own requirements for membership at each level that may or may not be beyond what the AAFS requires. The following is a general overview of the requirements of the anthropology section as outlined in the AAFS website (http://www.aafs.org).

Student Affiliate: (1) Must be enrolled in a graduate program leading to a degree in anthropology or a closely related field, (2) submit résumé outlining relevant experience or coursework, (3) must be sponsored by a Member or Fellow in the section.

Trainee Affiliate: (1) Must have at least a master's degree in anthropology or a related field, and (2) must be sponsored by a Member or Fellow in the section.

Associate Member: (1) Must have at least a master's degree in anthropology or a related field; (2) submit *curriculum vitae* that outlines engagement in forensic anthropology; (3) demonstrate involvement in forensic anthropology by submitting either two case reports, two research papers, or one of each; (4) two letters of reference with at least one being from a Fellow and the other from a Member.

Member: While already serving as an Associate Member the applicant must: (1) attend a minimum of two annual meetings (the meeting at which the title of member is conferred does not count); (2) submit for review two recent case reports (within 5 years), two first or second authored publications, or two evidences of teaching/applied anthropology.

Fellow: While already serving as a Member: (1) attend a minimum of three annual meetings (not counting the meeting at which the title of Fellow is conferred); (2) submit for review two recent case reports (within 5 years), two first or second authored publications, or two evidences of teaching/applied anthropology.

The highest level of membership within the AAFS is Fellow. According to the AAFS Anthropology Section, individuals permitted to achieve this status must demonstrate: (1) that they are actively engaged in the field of forensic anthropology via case reports, publications, or evidence of teaching since being elected to Member; (2) they have a minimum of a master's degree from an accredited college/university; and (3) they have attended the annual meeting of the AAFS a minimum of five times. Importantly, being a Fellow of the AAFS in the anthropology section does not mean that these individuals are qualified to practice forensic anthropology, as membership status is not a qualification. Rather, these requirements are a recognition of achievements that allow a practitioner entrance to the organization, which helps them shape the future of the organization, as only individuals at the level of Fellow can hold elected Academy or Section office.

Certifications

Certifications are a professional credential demonstrating an individual has the minimum required qualifications to perform discipline-related tasks. Certifications must be conferred by a certifying body. Currently, the ABFA is the only certifying body for forensic anthropology that is accredited by an outside organization; in this case, the Forensic Specialties Accreditation Board (FSAB). The ALAF, and the FASE have both recently developed certification processes in forensic anthropology as well; however, currently neither is accredited to do so, and the validity of such a certification could be questioned. For example, FASE has a "grandfather" clause that allows older experienced practitioners to gain certification without passing any certification examination. While this is how the ABFA started in 1977, this practice is no longer allowed based on the ABFA's current accreditation from the FSAB[2].

The primary tool used by the ABFA to assess if an individual has the requisite education or knowledge to practice forensic anthropology is the ABFA Certification Exam. While the ABFA has no official document regarding requirements for education or training in forensic anthropology, the ABFA application process and certification examination, which are required for all new diplomates, serves this role, describing the certification as: "the highest recognized level of

[2]Under ISO/IEC 17024.

professional qualification in the field of forensic anthropology. Diplomate certification is based on a personal and professional record of education and training, experience, and achievement" (http://theabfa.org/).

Basic requirements must be met before one can apply to sit for the examination and the evaluation of these basic requirements by an Application Committee serves as the initial evaluation process of an applicant by the ABFA. The applicant must be a person of "good moral character," a permanent resident of the United States (although, this requirement can be petitioned), possess a doctoral degree in anthropology (or a closely related field), and have three years of experience beyond the receipt of the doctoral degree. Once these requirements are met, an individual can submit an application to the ABFA to seek certification. The current ABFA application process requires multiple pieces of documentation: an application, three letters of recommendation coming from at least one current ABFA diplomate and representing at least two institutions, a current *curriculum vitae*, copies of training and proficiency testing logs (for now, these are only recommended, not required), and three forensic anthropology case reports with associated analytical notes and complete photographs that allow for a thorough review of the cases.

The case-related materials are blinded and then reviewed by an evaluative committee of ABFA members to decide if an applicant has demonstrated competency in the general practice of forensic anthropology and can sit for the ABFA certification examination. It is not uncommon for applicants to be denied the ability to sit for the examination, requiring them to update their application materials and reapply in the future. Typically, when resubmission of application materials is required it is based on issues of report quality and not with the *curriculum vitae* or letters of recommendation.

There are two parts to the ABFA Certification Examination: a written and a practical, both of which are currently offered once per year at the annual meeting of the AAFS. It is fairly common for an examinee to fail one or both sections of the examination in the first attempt and examinees may take the examination three times before having to reapply. The failed sections can be retaken the following year. Although, these exact requirements are likely to change in the coming years.

Here we will note that while the ABFA exists to "provide, in the public interest and the advancement of science, a program of certification in forensic anthropology" (http://theabfa.org/), the ABFA is not without its critics. There are many individuals practicing forensic anthropology who do not currently meet the ABFA's degree requirements for membership, having a master's degree, rather than a PhD as their highest degree obtained. Further, the ABFA requires applicants to submit their own case reports, implying applicants should be practicing forensic anthropology without certification. However, it is possible to submit "mock" cases that are not part of an official case file, or cases that were individually analyzed by the applicant alongside another Diplomate who authored their own, official case report. Additionally, the ABFA focuses on the North American model of forensic anthropology education and practice (e.g., requiring PhDs in anthropology), which actively excludes individuals from other countries with different educational systems from applying. Finally, in the past, the ABFA application and examination process had been criticized for its opacity; although, great efforts have been made in recent years to revise the process to make it more equitable and transparent.

Accreditations

While individuals become certified to demonstrate their qualifications to practice a particular profession, laboratories become accredited as a formal recognition that they are competent to carry out specific tests (Taverniers et al., 2004). Accreditation then is an effort to demonstrate minimum standards of quality and a dedication to quality assurance and traceability. Accreditation must be conferred by an accrediting body. The American Society of Crime Laboratory Directors/Laboratory Accreditation Board (ASCLD/LAB) is a nonprofit organization that accredits public and private crime laboratories. In 2016 ASCLD/LAB merged with the ANSI-ASQ National Accreditation Board (ANAB). The ANAB is jointly owned by the American National Standards Institute (ANSI) and the American Society for Quality (ASQ). The ANAB provides accreditation for various International Organization for Standardization/International Electrotechnical Commission (ISO/IEC) standards. The standards relevant to this discussion include ISO/IEC 17025 requirements for the competence to perform tests or calibrations, ISO/IEC 17020 requirements for the operation of inspecting bodies, ISO/IEC 17043 requirements for proficiency testing, ISO/IEC 17021 requirements for management systems certification, and ISO 15189 requirements for quality and competence in medical laboratories.

Laboratory accreditations are a relatively new concept to forensic anthropology, and the vast majority of forensic anthropology laboratories are not accredited. As previously discussed, the JPAC-CIL was the first accredited forensic anthropology laboratory in the world (Holland et al., 2008). The JPAC-CIL was accredited in 2003 by the ASCLD/LAB. However, because forensic anthropology is not a regular component of crime laboratories, which are the primary focus of the ASCLD-LAB, the JPAC-CIL was accredited under Crime Scene Investigation for their fieldwork and Trace Evidence for their laboratory work. The current form of the JPAC-CIL, as the Scientific Analysis Directorate of the DPAA (SA DPAA, also referred to as the DPAA-CIL or DPAA-Lab), maintains their accreditation under the ISO/IEC 17025 standard under the fields: biology, crime scene investigation, and trace evidence. While trace evidence accreditation is not a perfect fit for a forensic anthropology laboratory, the important components of any accreditation for a forensic laboratory, such as a laboratory manual containing all laboratory SOPs, and quality assurance (QA) protocol are consistent and maintained (for a more detailed discussion of the JPAC-CIL laboratory and QA procedures, see Holland et al., 2008).

The Medical Examiner's Office in Harris County, Texas, the HCIFS, currently houses the only other accredited forensic anthropology laboratory. The HCIFS was accredited in 2015 by the ANAB under the ISO/IEC 17020:2012 standard under the field: Forensic Inspection, in the category: Anthropology with the subcategories: Scene and Recovery, Human Identification, Biological Profile, Postmortem Interval, Trauma Analysis, and Medicolegal Significance.

The NAME has its own accreditation for Medical Examiner Offices in association with ANAB. In theory, a forensic anthropologist working at a NAME-accredited institution is covered under that accreditation and does not need their own forensic anthropology-specific accreditation. Part of the checklist to become NAME accredited specifies that the office be affiliated with a forensic anthropologist who is board certified by the ABFA. According to the NAME directory (mid-2017), there are currently 92 NAME-accredited facilities in the United States.

Regardless of the accrediting body, those seeking accreditation for a forensic anthropology laboratory must implement laboratory quality assurance protocols. Taverniers et al. (2004:535) defines laboratory analytical quality assurance (AQA) as "the complete set of measures a [n analytical] laboratory must undertake to ensure that it can always achieve high-quality data." Taverniers and colleagues (2004) go on to describe laboratory AQA procedures through the use of: internal quality control (IQC) procedures such as the use of reference material, exemplars, standardized charts, and performance checks; participation in proficiency testing (PT) for analysts; and accreditation to an international standard, which in the case of forensic anthropology, is typically ISO 17025. This AQA multilevel system is also explained via illustration in Fig. 4.1, recreated for forensic anthropology from Taverniers et al. (2004:536).

The importance of this hierarchical AQA system is that "using validated methods is the first level of QA, required within a system of IQC. The latter is needed for participation in PT schemes, which, in turn, form a prerequisite for accreditation" (Taverniers et al., 2004:536). In forensic anthropology the vast majority of methods used are validated independently by unassociated researchers and published in peer-reviewed scholarly journals; however, internal method

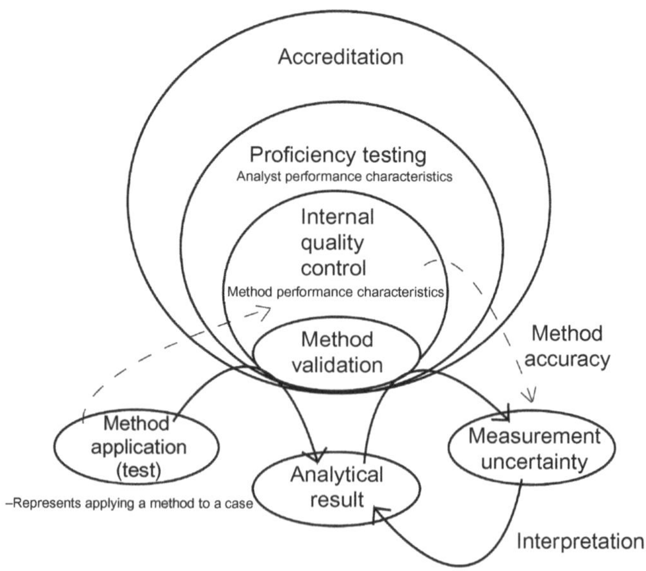

Figure 4.1 Diagram of laboratory AQA hierarchy modified for forensic anthropology from Taverniers et al. (2004).

validation procedures are sometimes used, particularly because they can be performed quicker than scholarly publication for laboratories needing novel approaches to casework. Depending on the accrediting body's requirements, a laboratory seeking accreditation must have the above AQA, or a similar system, in place.

An important component of QA systems are laboratory SOPs. SOPs are part of laboratory QA systems and represent controlled written guides or manuals created to set uniform expectations for the performance of specific laboratory functions (Manghani, 2011). Laboratory SOPs are the formal standardization of various laboratory practices and are meant to promote transparency, consistency, reproducibility, interchangeability, and facilitate communication and onboarding of new analysts (Manghani, 2011). Further, SOPs establish systematic procedures for all important laboratory tasks as well as what to do when required tasks fall outside of the purview of the SOPs. Laboratory SOPs are considered controlled documents, similar to any other authoritative forms, such as analytical note forms. Document control is another function of laboratory QA, which serves as a process for the consistent laboratory practices via standardized paperwork, as well as a process for updating or altering authoritative laboratory documents.

Finally, internal PT is a laboratory QA system to demonstrate competency of analysts to laboratory management, accrediting bodies, and other stakeholders. Performance testing of analytical staff is particularly relevant when analysts lack certification (Taverniers et al., 2004), such as in forensic anthropology where certification is not common or available to all practitioners.

STANDARDS BOARDS

As previously discussed, the SWGAnth was established in 2008 to develop standards for the practice of forensic anthropology in the United States. This working group generated 21 guidelines covering topics ranging from sex assessment, resolving commingled human remains, laboratory management and quality assurance, and a code of ethics and conduct; all of which were freely available online until the SWGAnth went on hiatus in 2014.

As mentioned in Chapter 3, Current Ethical Guidelines and a Theory of Ethics, this hiatus is related to the creation of the Forensic Science Standards Board established as a "key component"[3] of the OSAC. The OSAC is organized into five scientific area committees (Biology/DNA, chemistry/instrumental analysis, crime scene/death investigation, digital/multimedia, and physics/pattern interpretation). These committees are further divided into 25 subcommittees. Anthropology is a subcommittee within the committee of crime scene/death investigation.

The primary aim of the OSAC is to generate discipline-specific standards and guidelines within the forensic sciences (largely replacing the previous system of SWGs, of which the SWGAnth was one). While these standards and guidelines will primarily be dedicated to the performance of various analyses or the application of various methods, the OSAC subcommittees may also develop and publish their own guidelines for ethical practice and behavior. Unlike the SWGs, which simply disseminated their documents online, the OSAC subcommittees will submit their documents to accredited Standard Development Organizations (SDOs) in order for them to become professionally published and enforceable; with hopes that accrediting bodies such as the ANAB will begin to refer to these documents when developing their laboratory accreditation standards.

In a further effort to support accreditation standards, the AAFS created the Academy Standards Board (ASB), which is an ANSI-accredited SDO, supporting the OSAC effort by giving them a forensic-based SDO to work with for refining and publishing the documents generated by the OSAC subcommittees. Thus far the ASB has established 13 consensus bodies that represent various specialty areas within the forensic sciences (anthropology is one of these consensus bodies). Compared to the 25 subcommittees of the OSAC, there is much room for growth in the ASB consensus bodies if additional ones are needed. Currently, the anthropology ASB consensus body is awaiting finalized documents from the OSAC anthropology subcommittee in order to begin the process of comment and adjudication required before any documents can be published as a standard or guideline. These published standards and guidelines will represent

[3]https://www.nist.gov/news-events/news/2014/06/nist-names-members-first-forensic-science-standards-board

minimum standards and best practices within the field of forensic anthropology and are expected to affect accreditation processes for laboratories, and may eventually become a component of certification.

WHO CAN PERFORM FORENSIC ANTHROPOLOGICAL CASEWORK?

The best answer to this question (at least at present within the United States) is an individual who went to an accredited university with a focus on forensic anthropology education and coursework, earned a PhD in anthropology from this university, became certified to practice forensic anthropology, acts ethically, follows best practice guidelines and standards, holds membership in a relevant professional organization (e.g., the AAFS), and works in an accredited laboratory. All of these requirements (except the last three) are theoretically vetted under the auspices of certification by the ABFA, as this certification does not enforce best practice procedures as part of its ethical code, nor does it require that one also be a member of the AAFS or any other similar organizations, or work in an accredited laboratory.

The reality is that if we are to consider certification, professional organization membership, accreditation, and adhering to the SWGAnth guidelines (until the OSAC Anthropology Subcommittee generates published standards/guidelines) as stipulations for requirements to act as a forensic anthropologist, there are very few individuals who meet these criteria. If we only consider ABFA-certified forensic anthropologists, even these individuals rarely fulfill all of these requirements.

As of this writing (early 2018), there are 79 active ABFA-certified forensic anthropologists in the United States.[4] Of these current 79 Diplomates: 12 work for the DPAA, 5 work in other Federal Laboratories (FBI, National Transportation Safety Board [NTSB], Office of the Armed Forces Medical Examiner System [AFMES], and the Smithsonian), four work privately/independently as consultants, 14 work in a coroner's/medical examiner office, and the remaining 44 have a College/University as their primary affiliation (although many

[4]This number is expected to increase every year by approximately four individuals as some new individuals pass the ABFA Certification Examination and some other ABFA-certified individuals retire.

of these regularly consult with a coroner's or medical examiner's office). As previously discussed, there are currently only two forensic anthropology-specific laboratories that are accredited, and many medical examiner's offices are not currently NAME accredited. Further, relatively few practicing forensic anthropologists are ABFA certified. Berryman and Lanfear (2012) found that approximately 25%–50% of all forensic anthropologists who have worked, or are currently working in medical examiner's or coroner's offices have master's degree as their highest degree obtained, meaning they are ineligible for ABFA certification based on the current degree requirements. While it is unclear how many individuals who only have a master's degree are being supervised or peer reviewed by a PhD-level certified forensic anthropologist, the fact remains that as many as half of the individuals practicing forensic anthropology are operating without the possibility of certification. Such a situation is troubling, especially when considering some of these individuals may not be a member of the AAFS or AAPA, meaning they have no body of ethical oversight.

Moreover, as previously discussed, there are no standards for education or training in forensic anthropology, and many individuals with a master's degree or PhD without any training in forensic anthropology are performing skeletal analyses in a medicolegal context. This does not necessarily mean that these individuals lack competency to perform forensic anthropological analyses, but it does demonstrate how there are no means of regulating who is qualified to practice forensic anthropology.

If one merely looks at the terminal degree, is an individual who has earned a graduate degree in anthropology inherently qualified to perform forensic anthropological skeletal analyses? Almost certainly they are not; the specialization should at the very least be in biological anthropology (not in other related fields: archaeology, zooarchaeology, or cultural anthropology). Taking this a step further, would a degree specializing in biological anthropology be considered appropriate for an individual to conduct forensic anthropological casework? Or perhaps we can ask more specifically, is a bioarchaeologist (an individual who specializes in the study of human remains from an archaeological context) by education and training qualified to perform traditional forensic anthropological casework? While there are many commonalities between forensic anthropology and bioarchaeology, and the two can be complementary (Ubelaker, 2016)—training in one discipline does not make you inherently qualified to do both.

While historically many practicing forensic anthropologists were not specifically trained in forensic anthropology, this lack of disciplinary focus was due to a dearth of academic programs available. A recent review of the training and education of ABFA Diplomates #1–115 found that the majority of all the dissertations completed by these 115 individuals were bioarchaeologically focused. However, beginning in 2005, there has been a shift toward more individuals being ABFA certified with dissertations that focus on forensic anthropological research questions (Bethard, 2016). Since there is about a five-year lag from completion of degree to passing the certification examination, this finding is to be expected as academic programs have grown considerably since 2000. Also complicating these results is the fact that there are academic programs that offer forensic anthropology coursework and training by ABFA-certified forensic anthropologists that require, or strongly recommend, a dissertation focused on bioarchaeology rather than forensic anthropology. These programs argue that the dual training students receive makes them more marketable when looking for jobs and provides access to more potential avenues of research funding (e.g., Wenner-Gren, National Science Foundation).

All anthropologists are professionals; however, the specialized nature of the subdisciplines necessitates that their definitions of professionalism and subject matter expertise remain distinct. As bioarchaeologists are not inherently qualified as forensic anthropologists, forensic anthropologists are not inherently qualified to act as bioarchaeologists. Some individuals may be cross-trained to do both, and some individuals may be mentored and/or supervised by experts in multiple disciplines so that they learn the different approaches of each profession; but training in one discipline, even though both disciplines are similar in many ways, does not equate to dual competency. One way to remedy this situation would be for bioarchaeologists to outline qualifications for their discipline as well.

The ramifications of the differences in the disciplines are that if an individual without the appropriate education and training in forensic anthropology acts beyond their professional expertise, they are misrepresenting their qualifications and could potentially do harm to the case/investigation; and are thus acting unethically (see Chapter 1: Introduction to Professionalism, Ethics, and Forensic Anthropology, and Pellegrino, 2002:381). It cannot be expected that law enforcement agencies, attorneys, or the medicolegal authority overseeing the case be trained in examining the nuances of an anthropological degree to determine who is and who is not qualified to be a forensic anthropologist. There must be clear published standards that go beyond training in skeletal analysis as the work of a forensic anthropologist is becoming increasingly specialized and incorporates much more than the estimation of the biological profile. Forensic anthropologists may be asked to perform a search or recovery of remains, or to consult on analyses of postmortem interval and trauma. They need to be versed in proper documentation, technical writing, the intricacies of various law enforcement agencies, chain of custody procedures, providing expert witness testimony, QA practices, and proficiency testing to highlight only a few topics that extend beyond typical biological anthropology training. Currently the best way to demonstrate competency in forensic anthropology is to acquire certification by the ABFA or another certifying body like the ALAF or FASE. However, as highlighted, these certifications are not without their flaws.

FOR WHOM DO FORENSIC ANTHROPOLOGISTS WORK?

After considering forensic anthropology as a professional enterprise, and what qualifies someone to be a forensic anthropologist, it may benefit us to quickly discuss the concept of who employs forensic anthropologists. Forensic anthropologists, like all forensic scientists, have various *consumers* of their products (e.g., their analytical reports). These consumers can be broken into *customers* who are arguably "The People" (as in The People vs a suspect of a crime); *direct beneficiaries* such as the next of kin/family members; and *indirect beneficiaries* such as communities. Further the *client* (also a form of consumer) is considered to be the requesting agency and/or funder of the forensic analysis. A client could be a defense attorney, prosecutor, coroner, Medical Examiner, or family member. The importance in identifying these relationships is to ensure transparency of the scientific and evidentiary processes, and avoid conflicts of interest and the potential for misconduct, thus maintaining scientific integrity.

CONCLUSIONS

As exemplified by the NIST OSAC and the ASB, the forensic sciences are in the process of formalizing standards and moving toward accreditation of these standards and the laboratories where forensic analyses occur. As these standards are being developed, it appears that certification of practitioners of forensic science will become more and more necessary, if not a requirement to conduct forensic analyses. Forensic anthropology is included in this formalization and standardization, and gone are the days where any biological anthropologist, or even zooarchaeologist, could justifiably consult on medicolegal cases involving human remains. Presenting oneself as a forensic anthropologist requires specific training and education with both laboratory-based and academic experiences. The discipline is becoming increasingly specialized with expertise needed not just in examining human skeletal remains, but extending well beyond this initial training. Forensic anthropologists must be well versed in proper documentation of findings, various legal standards, certification, accreditation, and ethical considerations to avoid misconduct. As demand for the services of forensic anthropologists grows, it will become increasingly important that the discipline maintain standards and definitions for how to properly train someone to be a forensic anthropologist, who is qualified to practice forensic anthropology, and what is within the scope of forensic anthropological expertise.

CHAPTER 5

The Use of Human Subjects in Forensic Anthropology Research

Bones may be my business, but they're other people's families[1]

Clyde Snow

As anthropologists, we are concerned with the study of humans and must carefully weigh the ethical treatment of human subjects in our studies. As forensic anthropologists we are predominantly focused on the study of human skeletal material; however, it is not uncommon for research topics or forensic analyses to require the direct involvement of the living, or data (such as radiographs) on individuals who are still alive. Therefore, this chapter will outline legislation associated with working with the living as well as the deceased. This discussion will also focus specifically on ethical considerations as relevant to forensic anthropologists working with human skeletal remains in terms of casework, research, and publications. The chapter concludes with a proposed set of guidelines to direct ethical forensic anthropological research and data collection.

CURRENT LEGISLATION

Legislation of Research on the Living

The initial recognition that all peoples should be protected and afforded basic rights can be traced to the Universal Declaration of Human Rights. The declaration was adopted by the United Nations General Assembly on 10 December 1948 and serves as an outline of fundamental human rights that should be globally defended (Assembly, 1948). At around this same time, as the world was coping with the end of the Second World War, the United States and allies conducted several criminal trials. Among these was a trial of 23 physicians in Nuremberg, Germany who had performed experiments on

[1]Quoted in Nelkin and Andrews (1998).

Ethics and Professionalism in Forensic Anthropology. DOI: https://doi.org/10.1016/B978-0-12-812065-1.00005-1

human subjects (United States v. Karl Brandt et al., also known as the Nuremberg Doctor's Trial). The trial began in December 1946 and a judgment was delivered in August 1947. The defendants were found guilty of war crimes and crimes against humanity; seven were sentenced to death (Annas and Grodin, 1992). The trial documented human experiments that included the intentional infection of individuals with malaria to study treatments, subjecting individuals to extreme cold for prolonged periods of time, exposure to various poisonous gases, and experimentation with sterilization surgery and bone and muscle surgeries, among others. Many people died as a result of these experiments ("Trials of War Criminals Before the Nuernberg Military Tribunals under Control Council Law No. 10, Volume II," 1949). The data resulting from these experiments have been used in subsequent research; although, there is considerable debate over their continued use (e.g., Berger, 1990; Moe, 1984; Mostow, 2015; Pozos, 2003; Sun, 1988; Weitzman, 1990).

As part of the judgment rendered in the trial, an outline for "permissible medical experiments" was given that centered on 10 key points that would ultimately come to be known as the Nuremberg Code. This code was primarily based on the testimony of two US doctors, Andrew Ivy and Leo Alexander (Perley et al., 1992). These points included: (1) voluntary consent, (2) the ability of the experiment to "yield fruitful results for the good of society," (3) good experiment design, (4) the avoidance of "unnecessary physical and mental suffering and injury," (5) experiments should not knowingly result in "death or disabling injury," (6) the risk taken should not exceed the importance of the problem to be solved, (7) subjects should be adequately protected from "even remote possibilities of injury, disability, or death," (8) the experiment should be carefully conducted by qualified personnel, (9) the human subject should be allowed to stop the experiment at any time, and (10) the scientist must be prepared to stop the experiment at any time ("Trials of War Criminals Before the Nuernberg Military Tribunals under Control Council Law No. 10, Volume II," 1949:181–182).

Also relevant to the use of human subjects is the Declaration of Helsinki, which is the product of the World Medical Association meeting held in Helsinki, Finland in 1964. The declaration has been subject to various revisions, the most recent being in 2013 ("World Medical

Association Declaration of Helsinki: ethical principles for medical research involving human subjects," 2014). The document is meant largely for physicians, although "others who are involved in medical research involving human subjects" are encouraged "to adopt these principles" ("World Medical Association Declaration of Helsinki: ethical principles for medical research involving human subjects," 2013:2191). Much of the Declaration of Helsinki echoes the principals outlined in the Nuremberg Code, and highlights the need to consider risks involved and the rights of the human subject. The Declaration of Helsinki also calls for a review of the research by an outside ethics committee (in the United States this is the Institutional Review Board—to be discussed more later). The areas of emphasis of The Declaration may be beyond the scope of forensic anthropology; although, it does emphasize patient privacy and the need to protect confidential personal information, as well as the need for informed consent for "research using identifiable human material or data" except in "situations where consent would be impossible or impracticable to obtain... the research may be done only after consideration and approval of a research ethics committee" ("World Medical Association Declaration of Helsinki: ethical principles for medical research involving human subjects," 2013:2193).

In the United States[2] the National Research Act of 1974 led to the creation of the National Commission for the Protection of Human Subjects of Biomedical and Behavioral Research, under the auspices of the United States Department of Health, Education, and Welfare (DHEW). By 1975 a thorough set of regulations were created to guide research on human subjects funded by the DHEW. Funding would also be contingent on a review of the proposed research by an Institutional Review Board (IRB). The IRB is housed at the institution receiving funding and consists of at least five people with the requisite expertise to review the proposal in terms of science and ethics, as well as review the legalities of the research, professionalism, and community views (Glantz, 1992).

[2]This book is predominantly focused on the practice of forensic anthropology in the United States and cannot dedicate a substantial amount of material to legislation across the globe. For a comprehensive reference see the edited volume by Márquez-Grant and Linda Fibiger (Marquez-Grant and Fibiger).

One of the charges of this commission was also to outline ethical principles for research involving human subjects. The result was the Belmont Report, completed in 1978 and so named based on initial discussions that occurred at the Belmont Conference Center at the Smithsonian Institute. The report underscores three ethical principles to guide research that include: respect for persons, beneficence, and justice. The report also provides guidelines to define informed consent, evaluate risks and benefits, and ensure the fair selection of subjects (The National Commission for the Protection of Human Subjects of Biomedical and Behavioral Research, 1978). This report was meant to serve as a guide to the IRB process (Blacksher and Moreno, 2008).

With the creation of the Department of Education in 1979 the DHEW was renamed the Department of Health and Human Services (DHHS). In 1981 regulations as part of the National Research Act as well as recommendations in the Belmont Report were incorporated into the Code of Federal Regulations (CFR) Title 45, Part 46 (45 CFR 46). The next 10 years were witness to much debate and discussion over a final definition of this policy that would govern research on human subjects. Finally in 1991 what is now known as the "Common Rule" was published by the Office of Science and Technology Policy as subpart A of 45 CFR 46 (Porter and Koski, 2008).

The Common Rule constitutes the DHHS policy for conducting research on human subjects and thus bears consideration by forensic anthropologists. The policy specifically defines a human subject as "a living individual about whom an investigator (whether professional or student) conducting research obtains (1) data through intervention or interaction with the individual, or (2) identifiable private information" (45 CFR 46.102). The Common Rule also outlines how the IRB functions (45 CFR 46.107 and 108), and the criteria for IRB approval of research. These criteria include: (1) minimal risk to subjects, (2) risks must be outweighed by benefits, (3) fair selection of subjects, (4) informed consent is acquired, (5) informed consent is documented, (6) data will be adequately monitored for the safety of subjects, and (7) privacy of subjects is maintained through data collection (45 CFR 46.111).

In 2011 the DHHS announced their intention to update the Common Rule. In 2015 a Notice of Proposed Rulemaking was made available for public comment that outlined changes to the Common

Rule. Over 2100 comments were received from a wide range of respondents; these comments lead to a long discussion and a formal update to the Common Rule that will go into effect in 2018. The majority of changes are designed to streamline the IRB process and provide better information to participants; more exemptions will be made available to low-risk studies, consent forms will be shortened, and multi-institutional studies can operate under a single IRB review. Of note in the revision is the continued ability to conduct research on nonidentified biospecimens without consent, and the inclusion of clinical trials that are federally funded (clinical trials that do not receive federal funding are not subject to the Common Rule) (Menikoff et al., 2017).

Legislation of Research on the Deceased

The Common Rule explicitly states that a human subject is a "living individual;" therefore, research on deceased individuals is not covered under this regulation. In 1999 The National Bioethics Advisory Commission (NBAC)[3] found that the current "common rule" was ambiguous and "inadequate to ensure the ethical use of human biological materials in research and requires[s] some modification" (National Bioethics Advisory Committee, 1999:ii). These ambiguities are most notably illustrated in publicized cases such as that of Henrietta Lacks and Moore versus Regents of the University of California[4].

The use of human remains for research and analysis is a gray area that is not currently covered by federal policy. The use of biological materials from deceased individuals is identified by the NBAC as being part of the ambiguities of the Common Rule. Moreover, the NBAC (1999) states that in cases where research on deceased individuals involves identifiable data on living relatives, these living relatives could be protected under the current federal policy as human subjects.

In light of the lack of current federal policy and the NBAC findings, there are two main ethical (if not potentially legal) issues to consider when conducting research on the deceased: (1) respect for the decedent and their wishes for treatment in death, and (2) respect for the next-of-kin and their wishes for the treatment of their relative in death. There may be various religious or personal reasons individuals

[3]Created under the Clinton administration in 1995 and continued until the expiration of its charter in 2001. During its time, the committee produced six reports (Childress, 2017).
[4](1990) 51 Cal.3d 120, 271 Cal.Prtr. 146;793 Pc2d 479.

do not want research to be conducted on their own bodies after death, or on those of their family members. Decedents or family members may object to postmortem body modification, the research being conducted, the researcher, or the use of their tissues for gain or profit (Nelkin and Andrews, 1998).

In the United States, much of the legislation related to the recovery, analysis, and treatment of human remains is dealt with at the state level (Ubelaker, 2011) and will therefore vary from state to state. A deceased body is not considered property in the traditional sense in that there are legal relations between the decedent and a living person. There is, however, common law that helps guide legal disputes in treatment of the deceased. It is generally recognized in the United States that a deceased body is quasiproperty, which allows for the next of kin's right to sepulcher (i.e., burial), as well as the right to receive the deceased body in the same state it was in life (Nwabueze, 2007). The mistreatment of a corpse is covered in the *American Restatement of Law 2d Torts*, Section 868, "Interference with Dead Bodies." This section reads, "[o]ne who intentionally, recklessly, or negligently removes, withholds, mutilates or operates upon a body of a dead person or prevents its proper interment or cremation is subject to liability to a member of the family of the deceased who is entitled to the disposition of the body" ("American Restatement [Second] of Torts: Interference with Dead Bodies § 868," 1979). Civil cases have been litigated for violations of an individual's ability to claim a deceased body as quasiproperty. Cases have included claims surrounding four main categories: (1) establishment of burial location, (2) nonconsensual or unlawful treatment of the deceased (e.g., autopsy, embalming, removal of organs or tissues), (3) actions that caused a delay in burial (which could cause the next-of-kin mental anguish), and (4) use of the body for evidence in legal cases (Sperling, 2008).

As relevant to the forensic examination of human remains, an autopsy could be considered a violation of the right to sepulcher; however, it has been found that medicolegal autopsies (unlike organ tissue donation or private autopsies) are for the "greater good of the public" and cannot be refused by the family (Haden-Pinneri and Weedn, 2013:295). Also, as part of the autopsy, it is routine to retain tissue for examination and testing as relevant to the case. Medical examiners and coroners are subject to state laws; however, few states have specifically addressed the issue of tissue and organ retention of a decedent in a forensic setting. While there have been several court cases in which families sued coroners or medical examiner's offices for retention of tissues for testing, it is generally found that the testing was necessary and did not constitute wrong-doing (Haden-Pinneri and Weedn, 2013). In regard to forensic anthropological analysis, the processing of remains and the removal of soft tissue as part of the analysis of the skeletal remains could be seen as a violation of the next-of-kins' right to sepulcher, or even as destruction of evidence. However, these types of analyses are at the request of law enforcement and/or the coroner/medical examiner and are therefore typically under the same protections.

There are also ethical and legal considerations in the release of autopsy results. It has been ruled in a court of law (in *Reid v. Pierce County*[5]) that the release of autopsy records of a decedent can be protected in relation to the privacy of their close relatives. This finding, however, can vary from state to state, as some states view autopsy reports as part of the public record while others view them as confidential. Such state differences can make it difficult to handle the release or publication of autopsy findings. To address these state disparities the American Medical Association (AMA) formed a commission to establish policies on autopsy release. Their official statement is that autopsy reports are to be considered part of the decedents' medical records, and should therefore be kept private (Sperling, 2008).

A large part of the issue of research and analysis on deceased individuals is consent. In the case of forensic analysis, informed consent prior to death would be nearly impossible to obtain. However, there are means to provide consent prior to death for research and analysis. The Uniform Anatomical Gift Act (UAGA) allows an individual to donate their body for transplantation, research, education, or therapy in advance of their death; the next-of-kin is also granted the ability to donate the body if it does not contradict the decedent's wishes for treatment after death. The act also prohibits the trafficking of human tissues for profit (Champney, 2016). The UAGA is recognized in some form in all states; this act is important in a legal sense as it recognizes the body as having a property interest (Haden-Pinneri and Weedn, 2013). Within the United States, there are three types of organizations

[5]Reid v. Pierce County 136 Wash. 2d 195, 961 P2d333.

that accept donated bodies: (1) state or university programs, (2) not-for-profit groups, and (3) for-profit companies. While it is illegal to profit from organ donation, profit can be made on sperm, ova, hair, blood, and human bones; yet, sometimes it seems unclear if donors know of the profit status of the organization to which they are donating their bodies (Champney, 2016). The lack of transparency in these organizations raises ethical questions, and Champney (2016) has argued that anatomical organizations (e.g., American Association of Anatomists) should provide a certification or accreditation to ensure ethical practices are maintained.

In some cases, bodies are not willed, and the guidelines for use of these bodies is not always clear. In the past, executed prisoners had been used for organ donation (Caplan, 2011) and anatomy dissection (Jones and Whitaker, 2012); although, the ethics of such a practice is highly disputed. Nystrom (2014) argues that the use of unclaimed bodies represents structural violence against the various marginalized populations from which they are derived. Even today medical cadavers largely come from poor and/or minority groups in the United States and abroad, with as much as 20% of anatomical cadavers still resulting from the unclaimed in the United States and Canada (Dasgupta, 2004).

It is not uncommon for forensic anthropology programs to receive unclaimed bodies for use as educational anatomical skeletons. In such circumstances the medicolegal authority and their funding agency (usually the state) is responsible for arranging final disposition of the remains, which could include burial, cremation, or other treatments. By donating the remains to a forensic anthropology program the remains are curated for no or minimal costs and can much more easily be returned to the next-of-kin. Many decomposition facilities in the United States will only accept willed-bodies (i.e., they will not allow unidentified bodies to become part of the facility). There are ambiguities here in terms of working with unidentified or unclaimed bodies. If the next-of-kin has waived their rights to sepulcher of a set of human remains, then it could be acceptable to maintain those remains in a laboratory for teaching or research. Likewise a set of human skeletal remains that is yet to be identified could be held in custody by a forensic anthropologist for analysis (not educational purposes) as long as chain of custody is maintained so as not to upset the rights afforded to the next-of-kin. Data collection on unidentified remains may not be appropriate until identification has been made and discussion with the next-of-kin has occurred. However, situations may vary as will ethical considerations in the treatment of these remains.

RESEARCH IN FORENSIC ANTHROPOLOGY

Research on the Living

Much of the legislation on research involving the living will not apply to the research of the forensic anthropologist, as their work is predominantly focused on skeletal material of the deceased. However, there are instances where forensic anthropologists collect data on living individuals or consult on cases involving living individuals. While not an exhaustive list of forensic anthropological research on the living, several of these instances are described here.

Perhaps the most common type of research involving living subjects involves the collection of skeletal data from radiographic images. Such data can address various research questions surrounding growth and development, pathological conditions, secular change, as well as age and sex estimations, to name only a few. These projects are considered records-based research. The risks involved in this type of research are generally minimal and center on patient privacy; however, this research is still subject to the IRB process and, depending on the circumstances, may be found exempt or be subject to an expedited review[6].

Another example of forensic anthropological research that might involve living subjects is data obtained from dental casts. If the casts are already in existence, presumably the IRB process was completed by the original researcher, and one would need to ensure that their subsequent project would not violate that initial review, or should seek an additional review by their institution's IRB. If a researcher wishes to make dental casts of living individuals for future research, they must have the project reviewed by IRB, obtain informed consent, and also ensure that an appropriately licensed individual is involved in taking the impressions (in the United States, this varies by state). Finally, some forensic anthropologists may collect anthropometric data on the

[6]Based on Collaborative Institutional Training Initiative (CITI) basic course for biomedical researcher investigators. Accessed September 2017: https://about.citiprogram.org/en/course/biomedical-biomed-basic/.

living to assist in estimations of stature or facial approximation. Such projects would involve direct interaction with living individuals and would certainly be subject to the IRB process, and would necessitate informed consent and additional ethical considerations of the treatment of the data.

Medicolegal Setting

Forensic anthropologists routinely collect postmortem data on skeletal remains. Within the context of the biological profile, such data typically include skeletal morphology and measurements to aid in identification. Additionally, observations may include antemortem and/or perimortem trauma, pathological conditions, and idiosyncratic skeletal variations. These data do not necessarily remain in case reports and may become part of larger databases, either of the individual practicing forensic anthropologist(s), or of a larger research database (e.g., Forensic Databank, Macromorphoscopic Databank). These data are important for the creation and validation of methods within forensic anthropology, and such databases account for the many cultural, environmental, and genetic factors that can affect the skeleton.

Forensic anthropology laboratories and their treatment of skeletal data vary widely across the globe. Within the United States such laboratories can be found within universities, at coroner's/medical examiner's offices, or within broader governmental organizations (e.g., Smithsonian, FBI). Arguably the largest laboratory of its kind is that housed in the DPAA. This laboratory historically allowed mass data collection on skeletal remains of missing service members with data anonymization (e.g., McKern and Stewart, 1957; Trotter and Gleser, 1952), and this practice continues today (e.g., Brown, 2010; Burke, 2012). As data are anonymous, no permission is sought from the family members, although, it is clear the data are from recovered skeletal remains of American service members from previous conflicts.

It is worth noting that it may also be possible to collect data on collections of skeletonized human remains that are being housed in anticipation of forensic anthropological analysis. These sets of remains are typically encountered in mass disasters or human rights violations. For example, as a result of the tragedies in Bosnia, there are large collections of human remains awaiting analysis for identification. Similarly, within the United States, there are collections of skeletal remains of individuals who have died while crossing the border between Mexico and the United States. The scientific value of these collections should not be overlooked; however, these collections are of relatively recent origin that might bring up strong emotions to those involved, particularly the next-of-kin. There is no official oversight in these cases, and publications have resulted from such situations in the form of case studies (e.g., Kimmerle and Baraybar, 2008; Ta'ala et al., 2006) and methods have been developed using such skeletal collections (e.g., Birkby et al., 2008; Fowler and Hughes, 2017; Frutos, 2003; Kimmerle et al., 2008; Ross and Konigsberg, 2002; Schaefer, 2008; Schaefer and Black, 2005; Wright and Vasquez, 2003).

While the collection of anonymous data from human remains is commonplace, problems can arise when physical samples of bone are removed from the body for study with no intentions of being re-associated. In medicolegal contexts within the United States, resecting bone as evidence is fairly common; however, a number of offices, including the New York City Office of Chief Medical Examiner (NYC OCME), routinely create cast-bone specimens of remains that may have evidentiary value so that they can return the actual remains with the rest of the body. In humanitarian contexts the retention of bone is more problematic. For example, researchers may take skeletal elements to aid in future identifications through additional research or, they may take elements to create new methods within forensic anthropology in general. Problems develop when the elements are not re-associated/returned, lost, treated inappropriately, or consumed via destructive analyses. Such remains should have an additional level of oversight to ensure that families retain their rights as next-of-kin and that religious beliefs are not violated. Additional ethical reviews are warranted in these cases, and could be overseen by the group leading the investigation (e.g., the International Committee of the Red Cross [ICRC], International Commission on Missing Persons [ICMP], The Hague), or the home institution of the forensic anthropologist conducting the research.

Skeletal Collections

Skeletal collections exist within the United States, which are the subject of much research in biological anthropology. Historically, these include the Hamann-Todd Collection housed at the Cleveland Museum of Natural History. This collection was originally amassed by

Carl A. Hamann and T. Wingate Todd between 1912 and 1938 and consists of over 3000 documented skeletons derived from cadavers[7]. The Terry Collection at the Smithsonian consists of 1728 documented skeletons also of cadaveric origin. This collection was developed by Robert J. Terry in the first half of the 1900s and was originally housed at Washington University. The collection moved to the Smithsonian in 1967[8].

There are also modern donated collections that are either developed through the study of decomposition processes at various research facilities, or are donated directly to universities. Such collections from decomposition research facilities include the W.M. Bass Collection at the University of Tennessee, Knoxville; the Texas State University Donated Skeletal Collection at University of Texas, San Marcos; and the John A. Williams Skeletal Collection at Western Carolina University. At The University of New Mexico individuals donate their bodies directly for skeletal research where they are processed and curated in the Maxwell Museum Documented Skeletal Collection[9]. The same is true of the Boston University Donated Osteological Collection, where individuals can donate their bodies to become part of the skeletal collection for student and law enforcement education[10].

There are procedures in place at all of these institutions to gain access for data collection, and permission is routinely granted for legitimate research requests. Such procedures ensure the proper treatment of remains and equity in terms of research access across individuals and institutions. These review procedures are imperative to maintain ethical access to these valuable resources. It would be difficult for an individual overseeing these collections to systematically deny access to researchers or to promote their own research agenda. Generally, research at these institutions is nondestructive; research projects that require destruction of skeletal material (e.g., isotope or DNA analysis) will have significantly more oversight.

Presenting Results

There are ethical considerations when presenting data on skeletal remains and sensitivity must be maintained. First, data collected on

[7]http://www.cmnh.org/phys-anthro/collection-database
[8]http://anthropology.si.edu/cm/terry.htm
[9]http://www.unm.edu/~osteolab/coll_doc.html
[10]https://www.bumc.bu.edu/gms/foresncianthro-master-program/anatomical-gift-donation/

skeletal remains (whether from donations, casework, mass disasters, or human rights violations) should be presented with a professional and respectful tone. Not only out of respect for the decedent, but also for their next-of-kin, who may still be able to claim harm from inflammatory or salacious reports of the remains of their family member. It is not appropriate to incite sensational titles in presenting these results, nor is this the time to create clever puns or other "funny" titles to garner attention—the work should speak for itself (Passalacqua et al., 2014). One must also take care to not present photos that may be inflammatory (e.g., pictures of fleshed remains in a plane crash when not relevant to the overall presentation of skeletal data) (Walsh-Haney and Lieberman, 2005).

Publication of results from forensic casework may also present legal questions in addition to these ethical ones. It is important to ensure that the presentation does not interfere with the investigation and prosecution of the case, or the identification of the decedent. It is appropriate to check with the relevant legal authorities (e.g., investigator, attorneys, medicolegal authority) before publications or presentations are submitted. In many states autopsy reports, and possibly by extension forensic anthropological reports, are considered sealed and not part of the public record. So, great care must be taken in obtaining permission to publish results and to maintain anonymity of the case. It may therefore be necessary to remove nonrelevant information, such as the date of recovery, the county or state of recovery, the office in which the autopsy took place, etc.

It is not appropriate to post information, comments, or photos about forensic casework or skeletal material on social media platforms (e.g., Facebook, Instagram). Not only could such posts impede a legal investigation, the comments could be considered harmful and/or disrespectful to the next-of-kin. Even if the comments are general in nature, they could violate nondisclosure agreements and ethical codes to which forensic anthropologists should adhere.

TREATMENT OF THE DEAD IN NONFORENSIC CIRCUMSTANCES

Human remains may be encountered in various other settings that are not medicolegally relevant; although, they may come under the initial purview of the forensic anthropologist and one should be aware of how to ethically handle such remains[11]. Federal regulation on the treatment of remains thought to be Native American is covered in NAGPRA passed in 1990 (Rose et al., 1996; Ubelaker, 2011). Generally, Native American remains should be repatriated to the appropriate Native American tribal nation. The treatment of other historic skeletal remains that are not Native American or forensically relevant will vary depending on where they were found. If found on Federal land they will be subject to Federal laws, but if found on state or private property, state law will apply. The treatment of remains can vary widely across the United States, and ideally one should work with the State Historic Preservation Office to come to a consensus course of action that is not in violation of state and federal regulations and accounts for the wishes of the descendent community. The Advisory Council on Historic Preservation has created a "Policy Statement Regarding the Treatment of Burial Sites, Human Remains and Funerary Objects" that can provide guidance in various settings[12].

More generally the study of human remains in a bioarchaeological context is also subject to ethical considerations. There have been proposed ethical codes within the field (e.g., Larsen and Walker, 2005; Redfern and Clegg, 2017; Walker, 2008; Zuckerman et al., 2014), which serve as a good guideline for ethical treatment of remains in a nonforensic context. There is also a set of guidelines established by the World Archaeological Congress that outline the treatment of human remains (Vermillion Accord of Human Remains, 1989).

There may also be ethical considerations in the presentation or display of human remains, as in the case of remains that are plastinated (e.g., Alberti et al., 2009; Giunta, 2010), on display in museums (e.g., Alberti et al., 2015; Fforde, 2014; Joy, 2017; Sitch, 2010), or shared as images on professional websites or social media platforms. The Department of Culture, Media, and Sport (DCMS) in the United Kingdom developed *Guidance for the Care of Human Remains in Museums* (2005) that states the primary reasons for museums to display remains are: "to educate medical practitioners, to educate people

[11]There are many publications on how to differentiate forensically relevant human remains from those which do not hold medicolegal significance (Berryman et al., 1997; Berryman et al., 1991; Christensen et al., 2014; Paolello and Klales, 2014; Pilloud and Tersigni-Tarrant, 2017; Rogers, 2005; Sledzik and Micozzi, 1997), and will not be reviewed further here.
[12]https://www.achp.gov/docs/hrpolicy0207.pdf

in science and history, to explain burial practices, to bring people into physical contact with past people, and to encourage reflection" (2005:20). Importantly though, the DCMS guide goes on to state: "Human remains should be displayed only if the museum believes that it makes a material contribution to a particular interpretation; and that contribution could not be made equally effectively in another way. Displays should always be accompanied by sufficient explanatory material" (Department for Culture Media and Sport: London, 2005). To this point Alberti et al. (2009) disagrees, arguing it is the responsibility of museums to display remains in order to enlighten and engage with the public, so long as the remains are displayed "in ways which are designed to inform, involve, and interest visitors rather than to sensationalize" (Alberti et al., 2009:143). These guidelines are straightforward and also apply to nonmuseum contexts such as nonscholarly publications (e.g., promotional articles, social media platforms, blog posts, and professional websites) as well as other informative presentations to the public. Particularly in the case of professional websites or promotional materials, care should be taken when photographs of human remains are published to ensure these guidelines are followed. One must consider if the included photographs of skeletal material are actually necessary to portray the information about one's research or facilities.

A WAY FORWARD: CONSIDERATIONS FOR FORENSIC ANTHROPOLOGY

The dead may not have rights *per se* in the eyes of federal or state law—but should still be protected from harmful treatment (Holland, 2015; Kramer, 2015). In terms of conducting analyses on human remains for the purposes of medicolegal investigations, the forensic anthropologist will generally be covered under the same provisions as the medical examiner or coroner, in that analyses are necessary to resolve a case and do not require the permission of the next-of-kin. Forensic anthropologists working privately should ensure that the requesting agency has the proper authority to solicit testing of the remains before they are altered in any way (e.g., processing and removal of soft tissue or other destructive analyses).

The law concerning research of the deceased is ambiguous and currently does not have oversight. To address these issues, in 2002 the

University of Pittsburgh instituted the Committee for Oversight of Research Involving the Dead (CORID) (Wicclair and DeVita, 2004). The CORID specifically oversees research involving: (1) individuals who are "brain dead," (2) cadavers in a clinical setting, and (3) cadavers or other body parts/tissues from outside a clinical setting (Yasko et al., 2004:327). Similarly the Consensus Panel on Research with the Recently Dead (CPRRD) created a set of guidelines for work predominantly focused on cadavers or cadavers with still-beating hearts (Pentz, 2005). While these can serve as general guidelines for forensic anthropological research, they are still not quite relevant to work conducted on skeletons that might include destructive analyses and/or long-term curation. In fact, in its first year the CORID did not report a single request from anthropology (Yasko et al., 2004).

In the few publications that discuss ethical research in forensic anthropology, only two have provided guidelines regarding these issues. Walsh-Haney and Leiberman (2005) suggest that in a forensic context, permission should always be obtained to do research on human remains. Whereas, Holland (2015) provides ethical guidelines beyond expressed consent. Holland (2015) outlined four general principles for ethically working with human remains, which include: (1) respecting the decedent, while maintaining the next-of-kin's right to sepulcher in terms of (2) disposition and (3) condition; and (4) presenting results in a way that is not shocking.

As we have argued throughout this volume, forensic anthropologists interested in conducting research on human remains, must adhere to a set of ethical guidelines. As there are no such guidelines currently provided, we put forward the following suggestions. First, when possible, permission from the next-of-kin, or individual (prior to death) should be obtained prior to destructive tests, curation, data collection, and/or publication. We realize it is not always possible to gain informed consent as the decedent may be unidentified or the next-of-kin impossible to find, in studies with large sample sizes such permission could be burdensome, and in some cases it might be distressing to the family to ask for permission to study remains. We are not suggesting that research should stop if consent cannot be obtained for such reasons. Rather (based on Holland, 2015), if permission cannot be obtained for a legitimate reason, the researcher must ensure the following: (1) the benefit of the research outweighs any harm to the next-of-kin or the skeletal remains, (2) the right to sepulcher is not hindered, (3) published results are not offensive or inflammatory, and (4) data are anonymous and cannot be traced back to any living or deceased individual. As there is room for interpretation in this set of guidelines, it may therefore be necessary to develop an ethical body to administer oversight for research on human remains in the future.

CONCLUSIONS

In today's current scientific climate (e.g., NAS and PCAST reports on forensic sciences, NAGPRA), we cannot afford to appear callous in our treatment of human remains. As biological and sociocultural scientists, we must strike a balance between the ethical treatment of peoples' identities and the advancement of our discipline. Therefore, it may become critical for forensic anthropologists to institute such a set of ethical practices before one is forced upon us. Ideally, ethical oversight within forensic anthropology would be directed by the discipline itself and overseen by professional organizations. The work performed by forensic anthropologists is unique and falls outside the scope of most work performed in a clinical setting; therefore, biological anthropologists and forensic anthropologists are the most readily qualified to determine the ethical implications of such research. Although, review panels could have additional outside members to provide full oversight and ethical accountability.

CHAPTER 6

Reporting and Testifying in Forensic Anthropology

This chapter discusses forensic anthropological casework with a focus on analytical notes, reporting, peer review, and testifying. Emphasis is placed on analytical notes and the subsequent report. An analytical report represents the results of all forensic anthropological analyses while the analytical notes are the record of the work performed. Both analytical notes and reports are a necessity in forensic anthropology. However, guidelines for reporting are not widely accepted and even those used by accredited laboratories, like the SA DPAA, may be interpreted differently among and between accreditation assessors. This chapter addresses these issues and concludes with a discussion of the necessity of a peer review process as well as the ethical and legal considerations for the expert witness during testimony.

ANALYTICAL APPROACHES TO FORENSIC ANTHROPOLOGICAL CASEWORK

There are two general approaches to forensic anthropological casework: (1) Blind Analysis, and (2) Informed Analysis. The argument for Blind Analysis is that forensic anthropologists should perform all their analyses "in the blind," that is without any contextual or other potentially biasing information. This "blinding" allows analysts to perform their analyses and come to unbiased conclusions. Informed Analysis advocates that forensic anthropologists perform their analyses using all available information, so as to come to the most appropriate conclusions possible.

A potential advantage to working in the blind is that the opportunity for cognitive bias is lessened. Studies have found that when given certain contextual information, skeletal analysts provide incorrect conclusions that support the evidence they were given. Ultimately, this

Ethics and Professionalism in Forensic Anthropology. DOI: https://doi.org/10.1016/B978-0-12-812065-1.00006-3

information has been found to influence estimations of age, sex, and ancestry (Nakhaeizadeh et al., 2014a); and the interpretation of trauma (Nakhaeizadeh et al., 2014b). On the other hand, other anthropologists (e.g., Konigsberg et al., 2008) prefer the Informed Analysis approach, arguing that forensic anthropologists are "inherent Bayesians," and need the contextual information associated with a case in order to choose methods with appropriate reference samples so as to reach the most accurate conclusions possible.

The ANAB Accreditation requirements for forensic science testing laboratories requires "all test methods that involve the comparison of an unknown to a known shall require the evaluation of unknown item(s)..., prior to comparison to one or more known item(s)" (ANAB, 2017:12, Section 5.4.1.2). This language could be interpreted to extend to the requirement of blind analyses within forensic anthropology. Blind Analysis and Informed Analysis approaches both have benefits and drawbacks and are not necessarily mutually exclusive. For example, the SA DPAA takes the approach of having their laboratory analysts work in the blind, unless a laboratory manager decides to present an analyst with contextual information about a case for an appropriate reason. However, it could also be argued that this work is not truly blinded as analysts are well aware of the contextual time of death and the presumed biological profile of the majority of individuals analyzed at the SA DPAA (e.g., young male American service members from previous conflicts). Regardless of which approach is taken, practitioners and/or laboratories should be transparent and consistent, and outline their approach in their laboratory's SOPs.

Further, prior to accepting/beginning analysis of a case, a forensic anthropologist should consider their qualifications and competency to perform the expected analyses. As discussed in previous chapters, analyses must be within the scope of expertise of the analyst, and forensic anthropologists should not agree to take on cases that require expertise, equipment, or other technology they do not possess. Additionally, one must consider how the analyses will be performed. For example, the SA DPAA Laboratory Manual, SOP 4.0 (CIL Surety) states:

"[A]t the analyst level it is incumbent on the analyst to develop a test strategy prior to undertaking casework for a particular case. A solid test strategy contributes to the clarity of test reports, the efficacy of results, CIL productivity, and analyst professional development.

Test strategies are developed by the analyst using the following considerations:

- Investigative problem at hand (e.g., building a biological profile, segregation of commingling, excluding evidence from further case considerations).
- Completeness and condition of the evidence.
- Methods and models available.
- SOP limitations and considerations.
- Customer considerations (e.g., destructive testing allowed or not allowed).

The goal of the test strategy is to limit the tests to those that are the most probative and which yield the most robust results" (DPAA Laboratory Manual, 2017:4).

ANALYTICAL NOTES

What Are Analytical Notes?

Analytical notes (sometimes referred to as bench notes, examination documentation, or technical records) are notes associated with the analysis (i.e., testing) of a case and are the basis from which an analytical report is written. Analytical notes are the organization's permanent record of all observations, tests, findings, and professional opinions, performed during casework. While analytical reports are the presentation of the results of an analysis, all analyses and conclusions included in an analytical report must be documented in the associated analytical notes for that report. The ABFA notes that discrepancies between analytical notes and the report must be avoided at all costs as this is a quality assurance failure that can have disastrous consequences during testimony or laboratory accreditation assessment (http://theabfa.org/).

The notes serve as part of the case file, and as such are discoverable by legal authorities. To this end, analytical notes should be the work of a single analyst. If other technical analyses (e.g., scanning electron microscope, X-ray fluorescence) are performed by different analysts and are used in an analytical report, these notes should appear in the case file as a separate set of technical records. The forensic anthropologist can then reference those analytical notes as appropriate where they pertain to the findings and discussion contained in the analytical report.

Analytical notes must also adequately address the casework at hand. In other words, an analyst must be able to examine the notes of another analyst and write the analytical report from the content of these notes. The ANAB Accreditation Requirements for Forensic Science Testing Laboratories (ANAB, 2017:9, Section 4.13.2.1.1) states: "Technical records to support a test report (including test results, opinions, and interpretations) shall be such that, another reviewer possessing the relevant knowledge, skills, and abilities could evaluate what was done and interpret the data." Additionally, analytical notes must be traceable.

"Each technical record shall:

1. be traceable to a unique test record identifier;[1]
2. reflect the date(s) that testing was performed;[2] and
3. be of a permanent nature" (ANAB, 2017:9, Section 4.13.2.1.2).

Tests Versus Observations

Making observations and conducting tests is routine in forensic anthropological analysis. However, the differentiation between observations and tests must be understood by the analyst. The differences between the two are subtle and can sometimes be problematic. Observations are findings that are not associated with a method of analysis or statistical rigor. Observations will frequently not affect the estimation of the biological profile or assist in making an identification. For example, noting the presence of a button osteoma or the location and extent of taphonomic staining are both observations. While relevant observations are captured in the notes (e.g., the presence of a periapical abscess), not all observations necessarily have to be addressed in the analytical report. As opposed to observations, findings derived from tests are method-based and are associated with some form of statistical rigor. Within their SOPs (SOP 4.0 CIL Surety), the SA DPAA states a test is: "an orderly, predetermined, validated, step-by-step procedure designed to ensure uniformity and objectivity in casework. An analytical activity is defined as a test when it meets one or more of the following criteria:

- There is a set of test protocols or methods in place that must be followed by the analyst.

[1]i.e., the "case number."
[2]A date range is acceptable.

- There is a qualitative or quantitative result that lends itself to interpretation by the analyst.
- There is specific guidance on how to interpret the result" (DPAA Laboratory Manual: 3–4)

For example, the estimation of sex using the Klales et al. (2012) method generates scores based on pubic bone morphology as well as associated probabilities for female/male estimates, and, therefore, constitutes a test. Any tests and test results generated during the course of an analysis must be described and summarized in both the analytical notes *and* the final report. The reasoning and intent behind these requirements are that forensic anthropologists should not be applying methods without justification. Further, if tests are included in the notes and not addressed in the report, it could be construed as a concealment of possibly relevant evidence; such a discrepancy may be difficult to explain in court.

Incidental Findings

Incidental findings (IFs) are observations, results, or other findings that may occur during analysis but are unrelated to the goals of the analysis (Parker et al., 2013; Wolf, 2008, 2008). Generally, IFs are found during the course of research or casework, but are considered beyond the scope of the project, and often beyond the expertise of the analyst (Wolf, 2008). Wolf (2008:216) argues that IFs are intrinsic to human subjects research, and "the problem of IFs is serious, ubiquitous, and growing." Because human subjects are the primary source of analytical material in forensic anthropology, forensic anthropologists have the potential to encounter IFs in each human forensic case; however, IFs in such contexts are rarely, if ever discussed.

Within the forensic sciences, IFs are primarily discussed relating to biology and genetic analysis. In terms of forensic biology, IFs include issues of paternity/maternity or genetic predisposition to various diseases, the ethical question being: when a false paternity/maternity is indicated via genetic analysis, should the results be disclosed to the individual/family? Parker and colleagues (2013:225) discuss these issues in depth, and suggest that "the asymmetric distribution of risks and benefits from DNA identification provides strong support for adopting a policy of nondisclosure." The reasoning being, IFs have potentially serious consequences not just in terms of affecting families, but stigmatizing entire communities. Further, a policy of disclosing IFs when encountered may create distrust or fear in research subjects or entire research populations, adversely affecting participation in identification efforts. The ICRC mirrors such concerns regarding IFs and personal/reference information, stating such information "is a powerful tool when used correctly and dangerous when misused" (ICRC, 2003:12).

The goals of a forensic anthropological analysis may vary depending on the nature of the work (e.g., establishing medicolegal significance, searching for human remains, generating a biological profile, comparing antemortem and postmortem radiographic records); however, the traditional goal of a holistic (meaning all combined aspects) forensic anthropological analysis is the identification of a set of human remains as well as contributions to the cause and manner of death. Taking this goal into consideration, all observations or findings that do not contribute to estimates of the biological profile, the analysis of trauma, or the identification can be considered incidental and superfluous (i.e., IFs). While congenital or anomalous conditions (e.g., cranial/caudal shifting of vertebrae) may contribute to the narrowing of a missing persons list, or appear radiologically and therefore assist with radiographic identification, individuals often lack antemortem records or knowledge of these features. As such, reporting these conditions may unnecessarily complicate the report and introduce confusion among nonforensic anthropologists. Further, antemortem conditions such as indications of physiological stress (e.g., linear enamel hypoplasia, skeletal asymmetry, reduced vertebral neural canal size) are very unlikely to aid in the identification of a set of unidentified adult remains and once identification is made, may upset family members by suggesting inadequate care during the individual's developmental period.

In forensic anthropology the majority of IFs are observations and thus do not require formal presentation in the analytical report. Because of this, we suggest noting all observed pathological, anomalous, or other such features in analytical notes, but avoiding the inclusion of these features in an analytical report unless absolutely necessary.

REPORTS IN FORENSIC ANTHROPOLOGY

What Is a Report?

An analytical report (also referred to as a test report) is a professional document generated in order to convey information. Various types of reports exist within the framework of all organizations, and different types of reports exist to convey information at varying organizational levels and functions. Within the forensic sciences there is disagreement as to what exactly constitutes a report, whether it includes all the case documentation, or just the final summary of results (Epstein, 2017). Within forensic anthropology the report is the final summary of analyses, whereas the case file (or case record, case packet) refers to the entirety of the case documentation, to include the analytical notes, administrative information such as chain of custody documentation, and case correspondence. While the primary type of reporting performed by forensic anthropologists is analytical and based on casework, it is important to draw distinctions between the two main types of reporting, namely between analytical and informational reports.

Analytical Reports—Also called test reports, provide information, analysis, conclusions, and when relevant, recommendations (Guffey and Almonte, 2010). In forensic anthropology all casework involves the examination of evidence (e.g., skeletal remains) and analysis of the derived information to provide conclusions for the advancement of the investigation by medicolegal professionals and law enforcement.

Informational Reports—These types of reports provide information, data, and feedback from various sources. Importantly, informational reports lack analysis or recommendations regarding the data they provide. Rather, these reports exist to present individuals with the necessary data to perform their own analyses (Guffey and Almonte, 2010). Examples of informational reports are: various QA reports (e.g., audit reports), policy reports, progress/status reports, and white papers. Informational reports are generally uncommon in forensic anthropology; however, progress reports are often encountered when reporting on the progress made on a research grant to the granting/funding agency (e.g., the National Institute of Justice [NIJ]), and quality assurance reports are common in laboratories with QA systems.

Analytical Reports in Forensic Anthropology

Analytical reports are written by subject matter experts and serve as an authoritative record of analyses and conclusions based on professional knowledge and experience. They include descriptions of the work performed, results of the analyses, and interpretations/conclusions regarding the results of the analyses performed (Christensen et al., 2014). Analytical reports must be readable, representative of the analyses conducted, describe/explain the findings, and include conclusions, interpretations, and/or opinions in order to make them informative (Peterson and Clark, 2006). The format and information presented in forensic anthropology analytical reports vary based on each organization's preferences, goals, type of casework, and customer requirements.

Currently, there are no authoritative standards or requirements specifically for forensic anthropology reports; however, accredited laboratories are beholden to the ANAB Accreditation Requirements for reporting outlined in ISO/IEC 17025. This guideline states:

"The laboratory shall have a policy and procedure for the reporting of test results.

The procedure shall:

1. identify what will be reported for all items received, including items not tested, items created that were or could be tested, and for all testing performed (partial and complete);
2. if applicable, specify the content for simplified reports or an annex to the report
3. require the report author to review the test record and document the review if the author is not the person that performed the work;
4. address how to properly qualify the significance of associations whether by a statistic or a qualitative statement;
5. describe how to clearly communicate the reason(s) when the reported results indicate that no definitive conclusion can be reached;
6. require reporting of the initial database entry (e.g., CODIS, AFIS, NIBIN); and
7. require reporting of an association resulting from a database search (e.g., CODIS, AFIS, NIBIN)." (ANAB, 2017:20, Section 5.10.1.1).

While not binding, the SWGAnth best practice guideline for documentation states: "The test report should include results of each test or series of tests carried out by the laboratory, and results should be reported accurately, clearly, unambiguously, objectively, and in accordance with any specific instructions in the test methods. The reported results should include all information necessary for the interpretation of the test results" (SWGAnth, 2012:6).

Forensic anthropologists work in diverse organizations and environments requiring varied and unique reporting requirements. For example, not all forensic anthropology reports are written for a traditional medicolegal authority (coroner, medical examiner). Although they may be referenced by medical examiners, search/recovery reports are typically submitted to law enforcement. Outside of the United States, forensic anthropologists work for agencies such as the ICRC or the Cyprus Committee on Missing Persons (CMP), which, based on their operational goals, may require specific report formats or wording. Additionally, reports may ultimately be read by laypeople to adjudicate cases (e.g., juries, lawyers, law enforcement). Altogether, reporting must be balanced between using accurate terminology and avoiding the over use of technical jargon (Cooper and Neuhaus, 2000 and references therein; Meadows Jantz, 2013).

Regarding analytical report *content* the SWGAnth guideline for documentation suggests that all reports include basic administrative information such as the laboratory name and address, name and address of the client, and a description of the items received. Additionally, where appropriate, the following sections should be included:

- Minimum number of individuals (MNI)
- Biological profile (including sex, age, ancestry, and stature)
- Skeletal alterations (including antemortem and/or perimortem trauma, and postmortem damage)
- Traits relevant for identification (i.e., information that could be used to facilitate an identification if comparison records are located later)
- Identification comparison (a comparison of known antemortem records to the unknown records associated with the case) (SWGAnth, 2012:7).

Report content will also depend on the needs of the requesting agency or customer. For example, if a decedent has been identified, only trauma analysis may be necessary.

For forensic anthropologists who wish to become ABFA-certified, the ABFA requires that the following information be included in submitted reports: "Age at death, Sex, Ancestry, Stature, Time since death, Perimortem trauma, Antemortem conditions, and Postmortem/Taphonomic modifications." Additionally, the ABFA emphasizes that authors need to proofread for spelling, grammar, and professional language; avoid jargon or slang; properly cite references; specifically discuss the methods and criteria employed; and to include background/provenience information.[3]

Aside from the general content of a forensic anthropology report, there is some guidance for the use of various terms and phrasing. The SWGAnth Documentation guideline states: "When results, opinions and interpretations (however named) are included in the report, the basis upon which they have been made (i.e., supporting evidence) should be documented. Opinions and interpretations should be clearly marked as such in a test report" (SWGAnth, 2012:7). Recently the US DOJ proposed uniform language requirements for multiple forensic disciplines regarding reports coming from DOJ laboratories, which essentially covers laboratories in the FBI, Drug Enforcement Agency, and the Bureau of Alcohol, Tobacco, Firearms and Explosives. The forensic anthropology language requirements were "based largely on SWGAnth guidelines, a legal review of anthropology testimony, policy considerations such as those raised in the NAS Report, and the FBI Laboratory's current SOPs, capabilities, and limitations" (Angi Christensen Pers. Comm., 8/5/2016). The Proposed Uniform Language Requirements for the DOJ defines 10 acceptable practices and five unacceptable practices regarding forensic anthropology reporting and/or testimony. Examples for acceptable practices include:

> *"Human or Non-human Origin - The examiner may state or imply that skeletal material is* human in origin, consistent with human origin, *or that a material may be* excluded as being human in origin. *An examiner may also state or imply that an* inconclusive *result is the determination that there is insufficient quality or quantity of skeletal material such that the examiner is unable to determine the material's human or non-human origin."*

[3]http://theabfa.org/faq/applicants/

"Stature - An examiner may state or imply that skeletal material likely originated from an individual within a certain stature interval, which may include both a point estimate and the 95% prediction interval."

An example of an unacceptable practice is:

"Trauma Analysis - The examiner may not state or imply that a particular implement was the source of a skeletal alteration. The examiner may not state or imply the cause or manner of death based on skeletal alterations and trauma".[4]

PEER REVIEW

While systems to facilitate peer review have evolved over time, the concept of peer review for scientific or scholarly work has existed for hundreds of years (Rennie, 1999). Generally, peer review is encountered as part of the publication process for assessing the quality of research-related scholarly work (Berkenkotter, 1995). In such cases, peer review can be considered as the "evaluation of research findings for competence, significance, and originality by qualified experts" (Benos et al., 2007:145). Peer review (often called technical review) is also encountered outside of strict research settings, such as in the forensic sciences, as a routine part of quality assurance. In fact, peer review originated as a QA protocol for scholarly activity (Cicchetti, 1997; Rennie, 1999; Smith, 1997). Within forensic anthropology, peer review involves the review of evidence, analytical notes, and the draft analytical report, for consistency in reporting and accuracy in findings by a separate qualified expert. The peer review process typically overlaps the analytical process. Peer reviewer concerns and findings may lead to subsequent analyses and/or revised analytical notes. Therefore, peer review documentation is included in the case file, and should have an equal level of traceability and adequacy as the analytical notes.

In forensic anthropology the peer review of draft reports and their associated analytical notes is still not a widespread practice. This is unfortunate as the peer review process is inherently designed to ensure the quality of scientific information (Benos et al., 2007). The lack of a peer review process in most forensic anthropology settings likely corresponds to the isolated work environment of many forensic anthropologists who are often sole practitioners in university or medical examiner

[4]Documents can be found at this website: https://www.justice.gov/archives/dag/forensic-science

settings. These environments lack the QA systems enjoyed by other forensic anthropology work environments such as the larger applied laboratories (e.g., SA DPAA, NYC OCME, HCIFS).

Rennie (1999:7) argues that "peer review is the formal expression of the principle that science works best in an environment of unrestrained criticism." Because of the benefits of peer review, a number of sole practitioner forensic anthropologists have implemented remote peer review systems, where they pass electronic copies of notes and draft reports back and forth. These types of peer reviews are not a perfect solution as there is no party to adjudicate nonconcurrence on peer reviews, there may not be a practical manner in which to track and manage any changes to documents, and there are no mechanisms to avoid potential conflicts of interests between reviewers. It can also be difficult to adequately assess analyses on a case solely through photographs rather than by reexamination of the evidence. However, for sole practitioner forensic anthropologists, a remote system is better than no system at all.

While the need for peer review is evident, the current system is not perfect (Thurner and Hanel, 2011). As noted by Benos and colleagues (2007:146), peer review can involve a number of "issues including: reviewer bias, reviewer conflicts of interest, breach of confidentiality, disclosure of funding sources, and the proper venue for publication of dissenting viewpoints." Additionally, the peer review process prolongs the finalization of cases as notes, reports, and evidence need to be critically reviewed. This is especially problematic if the peer review process requires multiple rounds of review.

Even considering those concerns, peer review of analytical reports, like scholarly manuscripts, is best practice. In terms of scholarly publications, peer review has been found to increase manuscript quality and readability (Goodman et al., 1994; Rennie, 1999), and such increases in quality are likely reflected in the peer-reviewed reports as well.

TESTIFYING

The presentation of analytical findings via testimony is a potential outcome of a forensic anthropological investigation. Consequently, all forensic anthropological analyses should be performed anticipating such an event. When providing testimony a forensic anthropologist is acting as an expert witness. Unlike eyewitnesses or character witnesses, who testify based on their nonprofessional relevance to a case, an expert witness is permitted to testify to their casework based on their professional qualifications, expertise, and analyses. Of note, while expert witnesses typically testify in court, testimony may also occur at pretrial hearings, depositions, or a number of other nontrial court proceedings.

Expert witnesses act as impartial parties that would provide the same conclusions regardless of whether the prosecution or the defense requested or retained their services (Shuman and Greenberg, 2003). To avoid conflicts of interest and motivation bias (Koppl, 2005), the American Bar Association (ABA) has two sets of rules regarding the ethical payment of expert witnesses, the *Model Rules* (Model Rules of Professional Conduct) and the *Model Code* (Model Code of Professional Responsibility). The Model Rules state that expert witnesses can receive payment for preparation of testimony as well as court testimony, unlike other witnesses who can only be reimbursed for their expenses (Murphy, 2000:229). The *Model Code* further states that expert witnesses are not to be paid on a contingency basis (i.e., based on the outcome of the case), but instead are paid a reasonable fee (Murphy, 2000:229). Obviously, paying experts on the basis of their testimony has the potential to introduce conflicts of interest and biased testimony. Both of these rules are general and function similarly to a code of ethics for any other organization, so while they are meant to guide behavior and avoid misconduct, they are not necessarily binding or enforceable.

In many cases, expert witnesses are called to testify based on the relevance of their report to a particular case. In these instances, the legal team has little choice in who to include as an expert witness. In other cases (e.g., to challenge another report or for professional consultation), legal teams will choose the appropriate expert witnesses for their case based on their qualifications that can include professional memberships, publishing record, and the completion of peer-reviewed research. Additionally, subjective factors may also be considered such as credibility, integrity, and charisma (Cooper and Neuhaus, 2000).

While lawyers may introduce expert witnesses the ultimate decision about who can act as an expert witness on a particular subject is determined by the presiding judge. There are a number of laws and precedents at both the state and federal level to assist judges in making expert witness decisions. A great deal of information about the Federal Rules of Evidence and the *Daubert* and *Kumho* decisions (both federal level binding judicial opinions) has already been written (e.g., Christensen and Crowder, 2009; Murphy, 2000) and will not be fully revisited here. However, it is important to note that for courts following the *Daubert* or similar criteria, judges act as the gatekeepers for ensuring the validity of expert testimony (Grivas and Komar, 2008). In other words, judges oversee decisions regarding the reliability of an expert's testimony, which requires consideration/examination of their methods after their analyses have been completed. Essentially the expert makes the decision on which analytical practices to follow, but if this is questioned with a *Daubert*-type motion, the judge would then make a *post hoc* decision on whether those were the appropriate tests to perform and were performed adequately (Kate Lesciotto, Personal Comm. 10/23/2017). Therefore, judges who are typically not scientists and usually have no training in evaluating scientific practices are responsible for making decisions regarding the admissibility of scientific evidence. Potential expert witnesses therefore need to be prepared to thoroughly discuss their qualifications, training, certification, professional memberships, publications, work experience, and prior expert witness testimony to satisfy the presiding judge (Henderson and Lenz, 2015).

Even though forensic anthropologists may write many analytical reports over their careers, it is relatively rare for them to be called to testify on these reports. Murray and Anderson (2007) surveyed 118 members at all levels of the then Physical Anthropology section of the AAFS and found that only ~53% had ever testified. Further, they found ~81% of those who had previously served as an expert witness in court had done so 10 times or less over the course of their careers. While providing expert witness testimony may have been uncommon, the 2009 Supreme Court ruling in *Melendez-Diaz v Massachusetts* has the potential to change that. This ruling recognized the defendant's right to question the analyst who completed the scientific analysis, thereby requiring the analyst to personally testify in court (Bono et al., 2012). This ruling could require forensic anthropologists to be called to testify to their reports each time those reports are introduced into court.

To evaluate courtroom testimony of forensic anthropologists and legal challenges to such testimony Lesciotto (2015) reviewed legal cases from 1970 to 2013. The vast majority of forensic anthropological courtroom testimony dealt with: trauma analysis (including the analysis of toolmarks, such as saw cut marks), the biological profile, or the estimation of the postmortem interval. At much lower rates, individuals identifying as forensic anthropologists testified regarding photographic comparisons and footprint analysis, of which fall into niche areas that are outside of the general knowledge base of most practicing forensic anthropologists today.

When called to testify, there are multiple ethical considerations, many of which have been discussed generally in other chapters. When providing testimony, do not overstate qualifications or training. Nor, should the findings in reports be overstated and one need stay within the bounds of the analytical methods (Henneberg, 2016). Specifically for forensic anthropology the SWGAnth guideline for documentation states: "When testifying in court, practitioners should:

- Testify only within the scope of expertise
- Decline to answer if asked questions beyond expertise
- Testify accurately
- Completely disclose involvement in the case
- Be clear, straightforward, and objective in answers on direct and cross-examination
- Limit conclusions to those logically following from the data and analytical results" (SWGAnth, 2012:8).

In addition to these general ethical considerations, there are also legal obligations to take into account when testifying. According to the ruling in *Brady v. Maryland, 373 U.S. 83 (1963)*, prosecutors are legally obligated to report all exculpatory information (i.e., information that may lead to the defendant's exoneration) to the defense. This requirement could extend to all those who work for the prosecution, to include expert witnesses. Consequently, it is the responsibility of the prosecutor to ensure that experts understand their obligation to disclose all relevant findings that may fall under *Brady* (Bono et al., 2012). However, the defense is also ethically bound to interview the prosecution's forensic experts to ensure full disclosure is met (Roth, 2012).

The implications of nondisclosure in legal proceedings is illustrated in the Duke University lacrosse case. In this case there was potentially exculpatory evidence in the DNA findings, which the District Attorney did not fully disclose (Willoughby et al., 2012). Moreover, later testimony indicated that the District Attorney may have also directed the DNA analyst to exclude some exculpatory information, to which he agreed. While these actions could be interpreted as part of *Brady* the court instead focused on the timeliness of the disclosure, which resulted in other ethical violations (Mosteller, 2008). For this and other misconduct the District Attorney in the case was disbarred. The forensic expert performing the DNA analysis, Dr. Brian Meehan, was fired from his position soon after it was discovered that he may not have fully reported the results of his findings. In response to his termination, he filed a civil suit against his employer. The court of appeals ultimately opined that the "[p]laintiff's misconduct involves intentionally obscuring evidence and submitting an incomplete report in a court of law when clear explanation of the test results would have exculpated individuals wrongly charged. We believe public policy supports the conclusion that such misconduct is grounds for just cause termination of employment" ("Brian W. Meehan v. American Media International, LLC," 2011:26). Dr. Meehan in this case was not subject to legal ramifications, unlike the district attorney; however, he did face consequences for his actions and failure to fully disclose his findings.

While forensic scientists are not expected to be well versed in the law, they are expected to be familiar with legal requirements and to understand whether their forensic reports are subject to disclosure (Roth, 2012). Ideally the forensic expert will be guided to full disclosure by both the prosecution and the defense. However, it is remains the responsibility of the forensic scientist to be familiar with the obligation to disclose. Typically, expert witnesses have an obligation to fully disclose the following: any limitations of a method, any evidence that may negate other testimony, additional evidence not already presented, another witness's testimony or credibility, and any exculpatory evidence (Roth, 2012). Additionally, to avoid accusations of failure to disclose, it can be important to address reporting and testimony in laboratory SOPs (Willoughby et al., 2012).

CONCLUSIONS

Reporting and testifying are the culmination of forensic anthropological work and represent the presentation of analytical findings. Best practice dictates that reports are peer reviewed and supported by traceable analytical notes in order to demonstrate transparency and enhance quality and scientific accuracy. Reports are usually technical in nature and are written for the primary consumer (typically law enforcement, attorneys, or medicolegal authority). While no overall authoritative standards currently exist for forensic anthropological analytical report writing, the various guidelines and information available establish that reports have defined sections, which represent the common analytical aspects of forensic anthropology (e.g., MNI, biological profile, trauma, taphonomy, and identification). Further, these guidelines advocate for the inclusion of background and contextual information about the case, the laboratory/analyst performing the analyses, and statistical support for the various analytical conclusions.

Peer review is a QA process of examining findings for competence, consistency, and originality. Peer review is not a common practice among most forensic anthropologists who work outside of the larger applied forensic anthropology laboratories. However, the peer review process has generally been found to increase the quality of the final work product and is considered best practice.

Testimony is typically presented during deposition or in court and encompasses various ethical and legal obligations. While expert witnesses are called upon by the legal system the judge is ultimately the arbiter of who is qualified to serve as an expert witness. Although forensic anthropologists do not regularly testify to their findings, anticipate that this trend will change in the future. Forensic anthropologists need to be informed and trained as to their obligations for providing testimony especially regarding the disclosure of all relevant findings.

7

Discrimination and Harassment in Forensic Anthropology

Discrimination and harassment are relevant issues to all disciplines and areas of employment. In the United States both terms have legal definitions. Discrimination is disparate treatment of an individual or group of individuals based on perceived characteristics rather than individual merit (Merriam-Webster's Dictionary of Law, 1996a). Harassment involves persistent and wrongful subjection to "annoying, offensive or troubling behavior" (Merriam-Webster's Dictionary of Law, 1996b:222). The U.S. Equal Employment Opportunity Commission (EEOC) is responsible for enforcing federal laws surrounding discrimination and harassment in the workplace. According to the EEOC: "Harassment is a form of employment discrimination that violates Title VII of the Civil Rights Act of 1964, the Age Discrimination in Employment Act of 1967, (ADEA), and the Americans with Disabilities Act of 1990, (ADA)."[1] These legal acts provide a protected status for various characteristics that include: race, religion, national origin, sex, pregnancy status, age (over 40 years), disability, or genetic information. While the original Civil Rights Act of 1964 did not include sexual orientation or gender identity, the EEOC has since moved to include these as protected classes in line with various court rulings.[2] Discriminatory or harassing behaviors can include sabotage of work product, undermining work performance, workplace bullying, microaggressions, offensive jokes, ridicule or mockery, offensive objects or pictures, intimidation, threats, slurs, name calling, denying employment, and/or blocking promotion.

The topic of discrimination and harassment is incredibly complex and could certainly be the subject of an entire volume, instead we attempt here to touch on some of the more pressing issues within forensic anthropology. Forensic anthropologists need to be cognizant

[1] https://www.eeoc.gov/laws/types/harassment.cfm

[2] https://www.eeoc.gov/eeoc/newsroom/wysk/enforcement_protections_lgbt_workers.cfm

Ethics and Professionalism in Forensic Anthropology. DOI: https://doi.org/10.1016/B978-0-12-812065-1.00007-5

of their behaviors in various settings: the workplace (to include academic, laboratory, and fieldwork settings) and at professional conferences. Additionally, forensic anthropologists must take care to avoid discriminatory language in the production of reports and presenting research both to colleagues and the public. Finally, we argue that a more diverse discipline will help deter discrimination and harassment and will ultimately improve forensic anthropology overall; we address the current state of the discipline in terms of diversity and provide suggestions for steps toward inclusion.

IN THE WORKPLACE

Academia

Those working in a college or university setting in the United States will be subject to their own institutions' policies. If the institution receives federal funding, they will also be subject to Titles VI and IX. There generally is support from these institutions to implement and enforce policies surrounding discrimination and harassment, in addition to providing sexual harassment and diversity training. Professors who are supervising students must be aware of the policies currently enforced at their places of employment and ensure that their students know expected behavior and reporting policies. Harassment and discrimination training should be provided for faculty and students alongside other standard trainings (e.g., blood-borne pathogen training, sharps training, emergency and fire preparedness).

It is also worth considering classroom dynamics and the way instructors engage with students. Instructors should actively interact with all students regardless of gender, sexual orientation, social race, ability status, or age. This inclusion can generally be achieved through encouragement of all students. Such encouragement might require a conscious and concerted effort to employ diverse teaching strategies and engagement with a range of students (see Rocca, 2010 for a review of engagement strategies). However, the results of the implementation of these strategies will be beneficial to the entire class population (Wells et al., 2016).

Additionally, those faculty overseeing graduate programs and graduate students should not overlook the role they have in shaping the future of forensic anthropology; we cannot grow a more diverse ithout starting at the level of graduate school. A recent pproximately 6500 university professors across the country at they were considerably more likely to respond to e-mails Vhite male prospective graduate students than to any other req st (e.g., female, Black, Hispanic), even when the messages were identical (Milkman et al., 2015). This study highlights the challenges that some students face in applying to graduate programs; even before applications are seen, students may be discouraged from pursuing advanced degrees. Diversity can come in many forms, including individuals with various ancestries/races, genders, religions, socioeconomic statuses, who are differently abled, all of which should be considered when admitting a cohort to a graduate program in an effort to promote diversity.

Laboratory

Within the United States, most laboratory settings that employ forensic anthropologists will either be state or federally funded. Again these institutions will be subject to various state and federal policies governing harassment and discrimination. Privately funded institutions (e.g., Necrosearch and Forensic Anthropological Consultants, LLC) need to ensure they are in compliance with these policies so as to best provide a supportive and productive work environment. Active training programs in both public and privately funded laboratories for supervisors and employees can improve compliance with, and transparency of, harassment and discrimination policies.

While harassment and discrimination can take many forms in the workplace, one area within the scope of work of the forensic anthropologist that could present as particularly problematic is the peer review process. As discussed in Chapter 6, Reporting and Testifying in Forensic Anthropology, it is best practice for forensic anthropologists to peer review one another's casework. In many instances peer review is an unofficial professional courtesy, although, it can be more structured in large laboratory settings with multiple forensic anthropologists. The open review of casework can present an opportunity to undermine another person's work based on their religion, gender, sexual orientation, disability, or race. For example, a peer reviewer with biases toward individuals based on such characteristics might find more fault with case reports authored by these individuals. The peer reviewer might overly question methods and results forcing the author to defend or change their analyses. Ideally, peer reviews are overseen by a laboratory manager or director who can identify systematic discrimination in the peer review process and correct the issue. If a problem is identified, blinded peer review processes could be implemented, or additional workplace training on discrimination and how it might affect the completion of actual casework within the laboratory could be given. Trainings on microaggression (indirect, subtle, or unintentional discrimination) and promoting diversity in the workplace, in addition to having a clear code of conduct and detailed plan for counseling may help to deter such situations.

During Fieldwork

Forensic anthropologists and archaeologists routinely perform fieldwork both locally and abroad to conduct forensic search and recovery operations. Recovery efforts can be related to recent homicides, cold cases, natural disasters (e.g., hurricanes, Thailand tsunami), human rights violations (e.g., in Bosnia, Guatemala, Cyprus), or in the case of the DPAA, to recover unaccounted-for American service members.

Clancy and colleagues (2014) reported on a survey of scientists that perform fieldwork and their experiences with sexual harassment. In this study, 64% of respondents ($n = 423/658$) reported that they had personally experienced sexual harassment while performing fieldwork. Women were over three times as likely to report experiencing sexual harassment. Overall, women reported that superiors were the most likely perpetrators of harassment and assault, whereas men were more likely to report similar offenses from their peers. This issue was further highlighted in the field of biological anthropology by science writer Michael Balter (2016) who thoroughly presented a high-profile case of sexual harassment that occurred during fieldwork by a well-known paleoanthropologist.

More recently, Nelson and colleagues (2017) published an update to the original Clancy et al. (2014) study. A sample of the initial respondents was selected for more detailed interviews ($n = 26$). Overall, the study found that negative fieldwork experiences had an impact on careers mostly through limiting later access to resources and opportunities. Additionally, this study identified the need for clarity in terms of expected and acceptable behavior, and the importance of enforcing rules surrounding any deviation from these behaviors. They further make a call for principal investigators and field directors to ensure they have an enforceable code of conduct. Supervisors and leaders, particularly those in professional organizations, are in a position to ensure that there is a change in the academic culture to embrace codes of conduct, and ensure there are consequences for poor behavior and protection for targets and whistleblowers (Nelson et al., 2017).

Supervisors, assistants, and students must be cognizant of their behavior while conducting fieldwork (Wolft, 2005). As a discipline, we must also have clearly outlined codes of conduct and a well-defined means to report inappropriate behaviors—both locally and abroad. It is especially important for supervisors to be aware of these factors and to provide clear direction for how such situations are to be reported and handled. Codes of conduct are helpful in mitigating situations of harassment, discrimination, or other inappropriate and unprofessional behaviors while in the field. Such codes can erase any ambiguities or uncertainty about appropriate behavior and expectations. Participation in fieldwork should be contingent on the signing of such a code that would ideally outline repercussions for failure to adhere to the code of conduct, including the removal of the individual from the project at their own expense. These codes of conduct need to be tailored to the unique fieldwork situation. For example, the presence of graduate and undergraduate students, the nature of the fieldwork, and the level of interaction with law enforcement or the local community, could all require additional consideration in the code of conduct. However, as Nelson and colleagues (2017) suggest, the code needs to be enforceable and have clear consequences for violations.

An additional consideration is the inclusion of a diverse group of students in field school opportunities. As previously discussed, admitting a diverse group of students to graduate school can be difficult if we do not engage with all students. Such a process can begin with admittance to field schools. The Society for Historical Archaeology has a Gender and Minority Affairs Committee that provides awards to field schools for being diverse and demonstrating a commitment to diversity.[3] This program is an excellent step toward promoting diversity in field programs and could serve as a model for other organizations (e.g., SAA and AAPA).

[3]https://sha.org/committees/gender-minority-affairs-committee/

OUTSIDE THE WORKPLACE

Academic and Professional Conferences

Many forensic anthropologists attend annual academic conferences around the United States and internationally. Over the years, there have been growing concerns over the occurrence of sexual harassment at scientific conferences (Shen, 2015). The AAPA recently developed a statement of conduct for attendees during its annual conference, which must be agreed to as part of registering for the conference.[4] The organization has also arranged symposia and discussions surrounding this topic. The AAFS, on the other hand, does not have a policy on sexual harassment at its annual meetings. However, in 2015, in the Anthropology Section business meeting at the AAFS annual meeting, data were presented from a survey[5] about sexual harassment pertaining specifically to that conference. Results found that ~20% of females and ~3% of males had "experienced unwelcomed advances or requests for sexual favors" (M. Schaeffer, Personal Communication, 2017 Sep, 09). It is commendable that the section is recognizing harassment as an issue at these conferences even if they do not currently have an official statement regarding conduct.

While both organizations (AAPA and AAFS) recognize a problem, there are currently no means of action to resolve cases within these professional organizations. It is difficult to know if the present policies and recent attention to the situation are working to reduce harassment and discrimination at these events. These conferences represent an opportunity to learn and make new connections in the discipline. Harassment and discrimination in these settings should not be tolerated as it creates a negative stigma for the conference, the discipline in general, and can discourage diversity in our discipline. Targets of such behaviors feel immediate and long-term consequences of harassment, as it is not only personally traumatic, but the ramifications of reporting, not reporting, or being associated with harassment can have negative impacts on their careers. Professional organizations need to consider a means for immediate action that allows for the reporting of discrimination and/or harassment and thorough investigation of the reported event, as well as consequences, such as expulsion from the conference, exclusion from future conferences, or loss of organizational membership.

[4]http://physanth.org/about/position-statements/aapa-code-ethics-sexual-harrassment/sexual-and-other-harassment/ethical-conduct-during-aapa-annual-meeting/

[5]The survey had been conducted by Maureen Schaeffer, Natalie Langley, and Joseph Hefner.

LANGUAGE IN PUBLICATIONS, REPORTS, AND INSTRUCTION

Forensic anthropologists must carefully word reports and publications in such a way so as to not be offensive to the next-of-kin or other interested parties. We have already discussed the legalities and general ethics of reporting (see Chapter 5: The Use of Human Subjects in Forensic Anthropology Research and Chapter 6: Reporting and Testifying in Forensic Anthropology), but here we speak more to the subtle discrimination that may be present in the language we use in reports, publications, and in public presentations. Within biological anthropology, we are still feeling the effects of our academic history that was witness to times of eugenics and the implementation of scientific racism, particularly in regard to the discussion of skull shape (e.g., Blumenbach, 1775; Morton, 1839, 1844). In the not too distant past, words such as "*Negroid*," "*Caucasoid*," and "*Mongoloid*" were used to discuss generalized skull shapes and morphology, often in terms of race estimations in publications and reports. This typological approach did not appreciate the continuous nature of human variation, nor did it attempt to understand biological variation within a cultural context (which we argue the current forensic anthropology ancestry paradigm does).

We must be cognizant of our past and mindful of which words we choose to describe groups, populations, ancestries, or ethnicities in academic literature and case reports. Such awareness includes not only the words we choose to incorporate into reports, but also how we characterize populations or groups according to their biological characteristics, being careful not to fall into stereotypes about culture, gender, sexual orientation, socioeconomic status, or health status. As recent work has highlighted, individuals encountered in forensic anthropological casework are more likely to be marginalized which could contribute to difficulties in the identification process. It is therefore important for forensic anthropological casework to not contribute further to this marginalization (e.g., of individuals who may identify as transgender, foreign nationals, or from a low socioeconomic status) and to be conscious of how analyses are presented (Bird, 2016; Bird et al., 2017).

As a case in point, a term which could benefit from a more nuanced interpretation is *admixture;* often defined as the interbreeding and "mixture" of genetic material from two populations. Such a term can be problematic in forensic anthropology as we are dealing with multiple polygenic phenotypic traits that represent complex population histories and a broad swath of the genetic code. Trying to quantify population contact through various traits or stating that an individual is "admixed" based on a handful of traits can lead to erroneous results and overstep the limits of the data. Moreover, we must be careful in how the word admixture is used, as it can imply that there are groups that are not admixed, or rather, that there are source populations which are solely of a certain ancestry (Williams, 2016), which is not the case. Implying as such can harken to the concept of a "pure race," which is a dangerous notion to conjure.

The majority consensus in anthropology is that race is largely a social construct (Wagner et al., 2017), and that the human species is best described in clines with some patterned geographic variation; it is more appropriate to discuss *gene flow* or *dispersal* instead of *admixture* as that is ultimately what is being observed and interpreted. All populations show broad intra-variation that the word admixture does not incorporate. Alternatively, when talking about a single individual, as in casework, the appropriate term for the social race (e.g., based on the federal or state census, or how the individual may have self-identified) based on the ancestry estimate may be used instead of discussing the person as "admixed"—such an approach will aid, rather than convolute, the ultimate identification of the unknown decedent.

In addition to our academic work and report writing, we must be careful how we frame our discussion of ancestry estimation in the classroom and in public presentations. There are other groups willing to use and distort our research to promote their own discriminatory or racist agendas. For example, Panofsky and Donovan (2017) discuss the rise of commercially available genetic ancestry testing, and its use by white supremacists to further their objective of racial purity and superiority. Without caution, our work on ancestry estimation could also be distorted and used as a means to legitimize the concept of biological race or racial supremacy. It is therefore critical that we carefully choose our words, and how we teach and present the data to lay audiences. Our methods do not support the biological concept of race; they are instead reflective of microevolutionary forces that include gene flow, gene drift, and natural selection, as well as cultural factors such as positive assortative mating and geopolitical histories. It is important that these concepts not be glossed over or lost among students who might tend to fixate on the unscientific, typological approach using trait lists for estimating ancestry. Efforts should be made to focus on the concept of biological and social races as well as the extent of modern human variation prior to and during discussions of the estimation of ancestry (e.g., Hubbard, 2017).

PROMOTING DIVERSITY IN FORENSIC ANTHROPOLOGY

Diverse workplaces when managed properly with appropriate responsibility and oversight (Kalev et al., 2006) can increase productivity (Ottaviano and Peri, 2006; Saxena, 2014) as well as improve job satisfaction and reduce discrimination (Badgett et al., 2013). To this end we evaluate here the current state of diversity in forensic anthropology. This discussion begins with a review of a question that has received considerable attention in the discipline: "why are there so many women in forensic anthropology?" The question is evaluated as being inherently sexist and exclusionary due to the gender binary implicit in the question. We then evaluate the diversity of the discipline beyond gender, and end with a discussion on how to make the discipline as a whole more diverse and inclusive, which will only serve to improve workplaces and forensic anthropology as a whole.

Why Are There So Many Women in Forensic Anthropology?

In the recent past the question of the current abundance of women in the field of forensic anthropology has been posited in multiple settings. Before we engage in a discussion of why the posing of this question does not advance the discipline and can be seen as discriminatory, it is worth briefly investigating the status of women in the sciences, and specifically in forensic anthropology.

College and employment statistics present telling patterns in sex-based differences in the sciences. Male enrollment in college has steadily declined over the past several decades, from 71% in 1947 to 43% of enrollees in 2005 (Conger and Long, 2010). As a result, since the late 1990s, 57% of bachelor's degrees in the United States were awarded to women. Currently, women earn about half of the science and engineering bachelor's degrees and comprise half of the workforce in the United States. However, men occupy nearly three-quarters of the positions in science, technology, engineering, and math (i.e., STEM) (Beede et al., 2011; Houck, 2009; NSF, 2017).

While it is true that there are fewer women in the STEM fields, within forensic anthropology there is continuous discussion on the ostensible increase of women in the discipline. Donlon (2016) in her overview of forensic anthropology in Australia, highlights the fact that many forensic anthropologists there are women. She cites various possible reasons, to include: the fact that men are propelled to seek higher paying jobs, there is a female bias in studies focused on biology or social justice, and that the work is more laboratory based as opposed to field based (which is apparently more appealing to women). Or, that perhaps there is "a lack of discrimination toward women working in science generally, particularly outside universities" (p. 133). Another study, presented at the 2011 AAFS annual meeting also attempted to address the increase of women in forensic anthropology. This study cited the flexibility in forensics sciences that might be appealing to women raising families as a possible causative factor (Williams, 2011).

While there is discussion surrounding the increasing presence of women in forensic anthropology, there is little empirical evidence to support this claim. We attempt to remedy that here through various means of quantification. Early career forensic anthropologists are assessed through membership statistics in the anthropology section of the AAFS. The role of women in leadership positions is measured through Diplomate status in the ABFA, Section leadership in the Anthropology section of the AAFS, and recipients of the T. Dale Stewart award.

As membership within the AAFS is in constant flux, the statistics we present below are as of late 2017. There is a clear trend of substantially more women in the lower levels of membership (Fig. 7.1). Female Trainee Affiliates and Student Affiliate members greatly outnumber their male counterparts. As membership status increases and becomes more difficult to achieve (Member and Fellow), the numbers begin to equalize; yet, females still outnumber males. The only level where males outnumber females is in the status of Retired Fellow.

As of late 2017, 119 individuals have held certification from the ABFA. Of these 119, 50 are women and 69 are men. Overall there are more men; however, there are strong temporal trends in the male: female ratio of Diplomates (Fig. 7.2). The first Diplomates were granted this status in 1977. By 1990 only nine of the 43 Diplomates were women; by 2000, 16 of the 61 Diplomates were women; and by

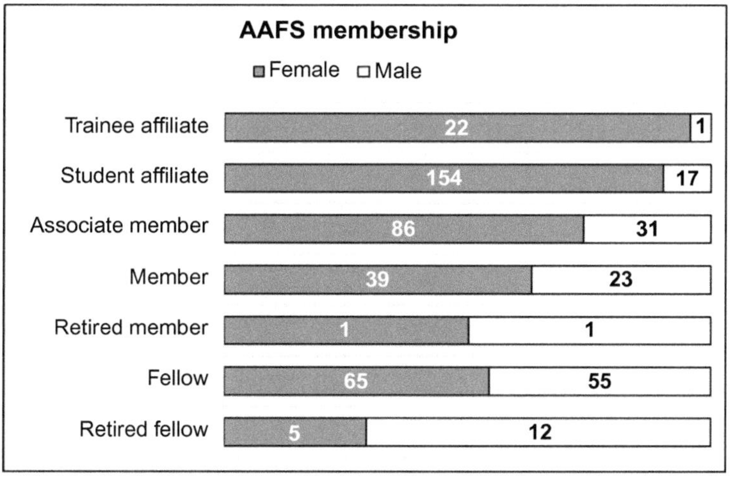

Figure 7.1 Numbers of males and females in the various membership categories of the AAFS in 2017.

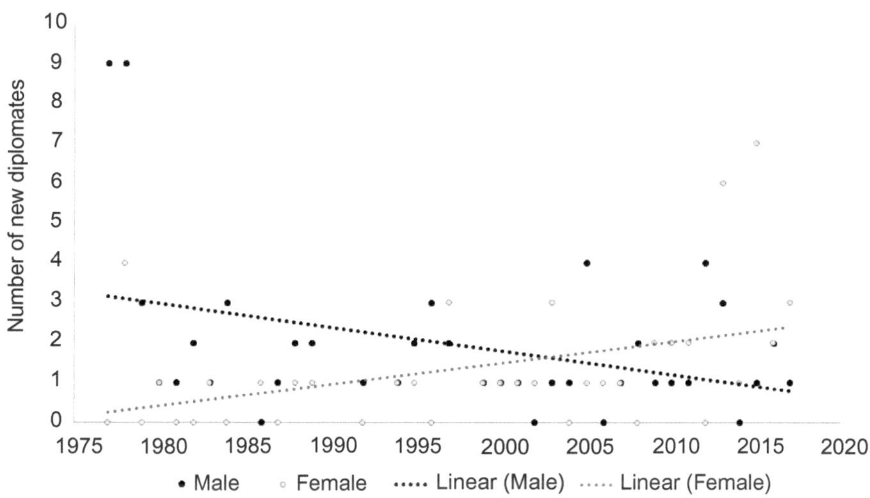

Figure 7.2 Chart of male:female ratios of individuals certified by the ABFA by year, with trend lines.

2010, 28 of the 85 Diplomates were women. It is really in the last seven years that women have gained a larger presence in the organization. Of the 34 new Diplomates since 2011, 21 have been women and 12 have been men. Of the current active Diplomates ($n = 79$), women slightly outnumber men (43 to 36, respectively).

A similar trend is seen in the leadership of the Anthropology section of the AAFS. Of the 34 chairs since 1974, 13 have been women and 21 have been men. However, since 2010, four have been women and only three have been men. The same pattern is seen in the awarding of the T. Dale Stewart award, which recognizes lifetime achievement in the discipline of forensic anthropology. Since 1980 the award has been given to 9 women and 26 men. Since 2010 four of the nine recipients were women.

While these changes over the past seven years indicate a more inclusive discipline, there is still an institutional past of over 30 years in which men dominated forensic anthropology and its professional organizations. This reality is most clearly revealed in the awarding of the T. Dale Stewart award, considered the highest honor of recognition in the field, which is still largely dominated by men.

While the increasing presence of women in forensic anthropology is worth examining, the question "*why are there so many women in forensic anthropology?*" begins from the premise that there *should not* be a balance of men and women in the field; therefore, it must be explained why women are present. All of these suggestions, and even the question itself, are subtle applications of gender discrimination and stereotypes. When this question is constantly asked of women, it puts the onus on them to explain their interests in the discipline and to justify their pursuit of such a career, and reinforces the gender stereotype that women should not be participating in the discipline in the first place. Such a discourse distracts from the positives of the situation and focuses on the past, in a time where women were generally pushed out of the sciences. It is time to stop asking for explanations for such inclusion and start pushing to seek ways to improve and broaden the inclusivity of the discipline. Instead of asking "why are there so many women in forensic anthropology?" perhaps we should reframe the question as: "how do we *keep* women in forensic anthropology?", "how do we *promote* women to positions of power?", and, perhaps most importantly, we should be focused on how we can make the discipline more *diverse* and *inclusive* as a whole.

In line with this final question, the preceding discussion focused on the role of women in forensic anthropology; however, this treatment also assumes a static gender binary, which in and of itself is exclusive. There is currently little research or data that discusses the role of the

LGBTQQIAA community (Lesbian, Gay, Transgender, Queer, Questioning, Intersex, and Asexual—and Allies) in forensic anthropology as a discipline, and how these individuals may be marginalized professionally. There are various organizations that are working to highlight the role of individuals who may identify as LGBTQQIA within anthropology as well as research in these areas. Such groups include the Association for Queer Anthropology (as a section of the AAA),[6] the AAFS Anthropology Section LGBTQ+ community and allies, and the Committee of Diversity—LGBTQQIAA group as part of the AAPA.[7] In an effort to improve diversity, the AAPA started an initiative to report on membership demographics. The results of this survey in 2014 are published online[8], and indicate that the vast majority of members are cisgender (with only 0.5% identifying as transgender). There is clearly more work to be done in this realm to ensure equity among all individuals, and not just those who identify as cisgender and heterosexual.

Why Is Not Forensic Anthropology More Diverse?

It should also be noted that the vast majority of individuals discussed in the previous section are White (i.e., ABFA diplomates, section chairs, etc.), indicating that most leadership roles in forensic anthropology lack diversity. The same is also true of biological anthropology in general. In the same 2014 AAPA demographic survey mentioned previously, the vast majority of members identified as European-American (87.8%). There is a glaring paucity of research exploring the lack of diversity in biological anthropology, and forensic anthropology specifically. Therefore, the following discussion will focus on anthropology more generally.

As previously discussed, non-White individuals face discrimination in being accepted into graduate programs (Milkman et al., 2015), which is likely to continue as they progress through their careers. Brodkin and colleagues (2011) conducted a survey of 105 anthropologists of color to explore their experiences as graduate students, early graduates, and as faculty. The study found that some progress has been made in making departments more diverse; however, departments continue to be dominated as "white public spaces" in which faculty

[6]http://queeranthro.org/
[7]http://physanth.org/about/committees/diversity/cod-lgbtqqiaa/
[8]file:///C:/Users/mpilloud/Downloads/AAPA_SurveySummary_ToItem18Only.pdf

and students of color do not have the same status or responsibilities of their White counterparts. Part of the issue, as the authors see it, is that anthropologists believe “that being an anthropologist inoculates one against racism (as well as other varieties of social stereotypes)” (Brodkin et al., 2011:554). The authors suggest that to actively combat discrimination, departments openly discuss inequality amongst the faculty as well as means to improve diversity. They further argue that to effect any sort of large-scale change, the AAA has to become involved and take visible and real actions to improve diversity within the discipline.

Within the two professional groups most relevant to forensic anthropologists (AAPA and AAFS) there have been recent organizational steps to improve diversity. Currently, the AAPA has a robust Committee on Diversity that includes various other working groups (e.g., LGBTQQIAA, women’s initiative, and international scholars). To improve diversity the AAPA was awarded three years of funding from the NSF as part of the Increasing Diversity in Evolutionary Anthropology Sciences (IDEAS) project.[9] The AAFS does not currently have a formal diversity committee; although, there is movement to create a Diversity and Outreach Committee within the organization.[10] Such organizations are great first steps to promoting diversity, and, as we argue below, it is imperative that professional organizations lead this charge.

Suggestions for the Future

To combat discrimination and harassment and improve diversity and equity in forensic anthropology, we must all be actively engaged in working towards this goal. In the United States, there are various protected classes that cannot be the focus of discrimination or harassment: gender/sex, religion, sexual orientation, race, national origin, disability, pregnancy status, or genetic information. Within forensic anthropology we can extend these boundaries to include individuals with various physical or mental health conditions. Additionally, we should make efforts to treat individuals at all career stages (e.g., students, interns, entry-, and senior-level staff) fairly and respectfully to ensure their future success. Everyone should be afforded the same opportunities in the discipline regardless of any of these characteristics.

[9]https://www.nsf.gov/awardsearch/showAward?AWD_ID=1516939
[10]https://news.aafs.org/section-news/do-you-want-to-help-aafss-diversity-outreach-activities/

To ensure equity in the workplace, various policies can be implemented to accommodate a range of life situations and to ensure employee/trainee/student success. Supervisors can provide flexible work schedules to accommodate various life challenges (e.g., child care, aging parents, and health issues). Additional mentoring can also be arranged to provide guidance for individuals who may be new to a particular workplace/laboratory setting, and unfamiliar with unspoken norms and rules (Settles et al., 2006). Workplaces need to recognize that the traditional career path of the White male does not fit everyone and that there are alternative paths to a successful career (Ceci and Williams, 2011). It is also important for supervisors and staff to be well trained in identifying and handling discrimination and harassment. Supervisors must ensure that complaints are responded to quickly and transparently, with no delays or secrecy. Good communication at all levels can ensure everyone feels included and their voices are heard. Assurances of a commitment to equity and diversity need to be verbally reinforced and modeled. Only in this way can individuals feel free to report instances of harassment and discrimination and can a diverse workplace be promoted.

During fieldwork and at conferences, a code of conduct with clear policies of behavior and consequences for noncompliance must be promoted. However, for these policies to function it is important for there to be a clear process to report violations; the responsibility of which should not necessarily rest on the target. If other attendees/fieldwork participants are witness to harassment or discrimination, it is their responsibility to speak-up as well so as to not be complicit in the harmful behavior. Additionally, the current stigma associated with the reporting of such events can be eliminated through detailed policies and training of all members.

To ensure diversity is promoted in the discipline, we may need to move further back to the education of forensic anthropologists. As anthropologists, we must educate our students, mentees, junior staff, etc., that diversity, in all forms, is what make us human and allows humans to succeed. In these educational settings, we need to cultivate a diverse set of minds to continue to innovate and expand the discipline of forensic anthropology. We need to model inclusivity in the classroom at all levels, not only by how we interact with students, but also how we present course materials and discuss sensitive concepts, such as race, gender, and sexuality. Further, we must mentor and encourage students early, taking into consideration all those issues raised throughout this chapter linked to diversity and inclusion. Especially considering the importance of equity in access to various opportunities and career paths in order to foster their interest and potential, not just GPAs and GRE scores. There are many winding paths to an advanced degree, all of which deserve consideration.

Finally, to genuinely enact change, various professional organizations must act as disciplinary leaders. The AAPA is a model for how this work can be done: they have an extensive Committee on Diversity and have secured funding to improve diversity efforts. They hold annual diversity workshops and are working toward demographic monitoring so that results of these efforts can be quantified and the success of these efforts measured. They contain a policy on behavior at annual conferences, although there is currently no means to enforce misconduct. We hope that the AAFS will move forward with their proposal to institute a similar committee and commit to a culture of inclusion and diversity. However, we further argue that both groups should include actionable consequences for discriminatory or harassing behaviors in professional settings.

CONCLUSIONS

Harassment and discrimination are common throughout the sciences; forensic anthropology is no exception. With varied power dynamics between advisors and students, and junior and senior professionals, as well as the multitude of issues that can arise in fieldwork situations, it is important for there to be open and honest discussions about harassment and discrimination in forensic anthropology to minimize these occurrences. In recent years, positive actions have occurred toward constructing a more inclusive forensic anthropology, but there is much room for improvement. The presence of White women in the field has increased, but there has not been concomitant growth in other aspects of diversity within the discipline. We all have unconscious biases—but, it is important to work on acknowledging them and not allow these biases to have a negative impact on the future of the discipline. By being mindful and challenging these biases, we can create a more inclusive discipline. As a more diverse and equitable discipline, we can grow both academically and personally in ways that will only improve forensic anthropology as a whole.

CHAPTER 8

Looking Backward and Thinking Forward

Throughout this volume we have attempted to present various ethical and professional issues within the context of the current practice of forensic anthropology. We argue that while the discipline of forensic anthropology has gone through significant changes since its official start in the 1970s, we have further to go in terms of professionalism and ethical practice.

This book began with a discussion of the need for the ethical practice of forensic anthropology (Chapter 2: The Need for Professional Ethics). Unethical behavior negatively impacts all practitioners as well as the discipline itself. Ethical codes are necessary as they codify which behaviors a discipline considers to be beneficial and which behaviors are detrimental. We also discussed transparency, misconduct, and conflicts of interest within the context of scientific integrity; the maintenance of which is essential to the practice of all professional science.

There are currently several ethical codes within anthropology that are outlined in Chapter 3, Current Ethical Guidelines and a Theory of Ethics. Most relevant to forensic anthropologists are either the ABFA's ethical code or that of the SWGAnth. However, we argued that none of the current ethical codes for forensic anthropologists are based on a theory of ethics, nor are they widely applicable. We further argue that a true ethical code for forensic anthropology must incorporate a theory of ethics informed by aspects from anthropology, medicine, and science. Forensic anthropology needs an ethical code that is enforceable and not tied to a single organization, unless that organization is a certification or accreditation body to which all practicing forensic anthropologists must be beholden.

Following Pellegrino (2002), Chapter 4, Defining the Role of the Forensic Anthropologist, discussed forensic anthropology as a profession by meeting several structural requirements. While many of these structural requirements are met, the discipline is lacking in several criteria, as clear standards for ethical behavior, education, and the performance

Ethics and Professionalism in Forensic Anthropology. DOI: https://doi.org/10.1016/B978-0-12-812065-1.00008-7

of forensic anthropology have not been expressly delineated or widely accepted. The reality of this situation is that analysts without the requisite education, training, professional memberships, or QA practices are performing forensic anthropological casework. We conclude the chapter with various solutions to address these issues of professionalism in forensic anthropology.

We then turned to the current legislation surrounding the use of human subjects in scientific research and its relevance to forensic anthropology (Chapter 5: The Use of Human Subjects in Forensic Anthropology Research). This discussion also covered the legislation of working with deceased human subjects, and ethical concerns surrounding the publication and use of these data for research. As forensic anthropology is currently lacking guidelines and oversight for research using human remains, we offer broad ethical guidelines.

In Chapter 6, Reporting and Testifying in Forensic Anthropology, we discussed analytical notes, reports, peer review, and testifying. The use of analytical notes supports quality assurance protocols and traceability. There are no current standards for writing forensic anthropology reports, although several guidelines do exist. The peer review of cases, to include analytical notes and reports, is another form of quality assurance that is only beginning to become commonplace in forensic anthropology. Outside of larger forensic anthropology laboratories (e.g., DPAA, NYC OCME, HCIFS), the practice of peer review is rare. Most forensic anthropologists work in isolation from other anthropologists and thus can only have their work reviewed remotely. The chapter concludes with a discussion of various legal and ethical considerations when providing testimony to include disclosure and avoiding any bias.

In the final substantive chapter (Chapter 7: Discrimination and Harassment in Forensic Anthropology) issues of harassment and discrimination within anthropology were addressed. With the potential for discrimination and harassment in various settings, it is important for there to be open and honest discussions as well as actionable codes of conduct to minimalize these occurrences. As a discipline dedicated to the understanding of human diversity, anthropologists are well suited for combating such issues. For this same reason, it is especially disappointing when anthropologists perform these negative behaviors, witness these behaviors and take no action, or lack means to enforce penalties toward the offenders. This chapter also offers various suggestions for how the discipline can become more diverse and inclusive.

Ethics and professionalism are not issues currently at the forefront of forensic anthropology, although, they clearly hold an important role. The forensic sciences are currently at a turning point, requiring the development of various professional procedures (e.g., certification, accreditation) with the goal of increasing quality and transparency of the forensic sciences in general. Forensic anthropology training programs do not typically include any formal ethics or professionalism coursework outside of the occasional lecture on NAGPRA or an IRB workshop. It is our hope that the many topics and issues we have discussed in this volume will demonstrate the need for forensic anthropologists to consider ethics an important part of the discipline. We also hope that our brief discussions here will produce other productive discussions between individuals and organizations.

We hope this volume has been informative and thought provoking. When it comes to ethical dilemmas, there are not always correct answers. In such situations the best we can do is to follow our ethical codes and act in a way that benefits all of forensic anthropology, to include the products (i.e., reports and publications), its practitioners (i.e., forensic anthropologists), the discipline as a whole, and other interested parties (e.g., next-of-kin, law enforcement). When evaluating a potential ethical issue, we suggest considering the issues of *context* and *consent*. What may be appropriate in one context, may be misconduct in another. Additionally, what may seem inflammatory or inappropriate may be supported via consent.

Looking forward, the future of forensic anthropology as a profession is only as bright as our dedication to scientific integrity, the practice of good science; supporting the various procedures that ensure quality; and creating an inclusive, welcoming, and diverse field of professional practitioners.

APPENDIX *A*

Acronyms

AAA	American Anthropological Association
AAFS	American Academy of Forensic Sciences
AAPA	American Association of Physical Anthropologists
AB	Accreditation Body
ABA	American Bar Association
ABFA	American Board of Forensic Anthropology
ADA	Americans with Disabilities Act
AFIS	Automated Fingerprint Information Systems
AFME	Armed Forces Medical Examiner
AFMES	Armed Forces Medical Examiner System
ALAF	Asociación Latinoamericana de Antropología Forense/ Latin American Forensic Anthropology Association
AMA	American Medical Association
ANAB	ANSI-ASQ National Accreditation Board
ANSI	American National Standards Institute
AQA	Analytical Quality Assurance
ASB	AAFS Standards Board
ASCLD	American Society of Crime Lab Directors
ASCLD/ LAB	American Society of Crime Lab Directors/Laboratory Accreditation Board
ASQ	American Society for Quality
ATF	Bureau of Alcohol, Tobacco, Firearms and Explosives
BABAO	British Association for Biological Anthropology and Osteoarchaeology
BAFA	British Association for Forensic Anthropology
BAHI	British Association for Human Identification
CB	Certification Body
CFR	Code of Federal Regulations
CIfA	Chartered Institute for Archaeologists
CIL	Central Identification Laboratory
CMP	Committee on Missing Persons
CODIS	Combined DNA Index System

CORID	Committee for Oversight of Research Involving the Dead
CPRRD	Consensus Panel on Research with the Recently Dead
DCMS	Department of Culture, Media, and Sport
DEA	Drug Enforcement Agency
DHEW	Department of Health, Education, and Welfare
DHHS	Department of Health and Human Services
DNA	Deoxyribonucleic acid
DOJ	Department of Justice
DPAA	Defense POW/MIA Accounting Agency
EEOC	Equal Employment Opportunity Commission
FASE	Forensic Anthropology Society of Europe
FBI	Federal Bureau of Investigation
FEPAC	Forensic Science Education Programs Accreditation Commission
FSAB	Forensic Specialties Accreditation Board
HCIFS	The Harris County Institute of Forensic Sciences
IALM	International Academy of Legal Medicine
ICMP	International Commission on Missing Persons
ICRC	International Committee of the Red Cross
IEC	International Electrotechnical Commission
IF	Incidental Finding
IQC	Internal Quality Control
IRB	Institutional Review Board
ISO	International Organization for Standardization
JPAC	Joint POW-MIA Accounting Agency
JPAC-CIL	Joint POW-MIA Accounting Agency-Central Identification Laboratory
ME	Medical Examiner
MNI	Minimum Number of Individuals
MOU	Memorandum of Understanding
NAGPRA	Native American Grave Protection and Repatriation Act
NAME	National Association of Medical Examiner's
NamUs	National Missing and Unidentified Persons System
NAPA	National Association for the Practice of Anthropology
NAS	National Academy of Sciences
NBAC	National Bioethics Advisory Commission
NCEPRFS	National Code of Ethics and Professional Responsibility for the Forensic Sciences

NCFS	National Commission on Forensic Science
NIBIN	National Database of Digital Images
NIFS	National Institute of Forensic Sciences
NIJ	National Institute of Justice
NIST	National Institute of Standards and Technology
NSF	National Science Foundation
NSHE	Nevada System of Higher Education
NTSB	National Transportation Safety Board
NYC OCME	New York City Office of Chief Medical Examiner
ORI	Office of Research Integrity
OSAC	Organization of Scientific Area Committees
PCAST	President's Council of Advisors on Science and Technology
PCOME	Pima County Office of the Medical Examiner
PRR	Principles of Professional Responsibility
PT	Proficiency Testing
QA	Quality Assurance
RAI	Royal Anthropological Institute
SA DPAA	Scientific Analysis Directorate of the Defense POW/MIA Accounting Agency
SAA	Society for American Archaeology
SDO	Standard Development Organization
SOFA	Society of Forensic Anthropologists
SOP	Standard Operating Procedure
STEM	Science, Technology, Engineering, and Math
SWG	Scientific Working Group
SWGAnth	Scientific Working Group for forensic anthropology
UAGA	Uniform Anatomical Gift Act
UK	United Kingdom
US	United States (of America)
WAC	World Archaeological Congress

APPENDIX B

SWGAnth Guidelines

SWGANTH CODE OF ETHICS AND CONDUCT

Issue date: Jan 05, 2013

Spirit and Intent

The profession of Forensic Anthropology demands a high level of scientific competence and an ethical practice that is beyond reproach. Forensic anthropologists shall maintain a high level of personal and professional integrity in accordance with the trust placed upon them by the government, the legal system, and the public.

Purpose and Scope

Because the search for and the recovery, analysis, and identification of human remains are complex procedures, often performed for diverse jurisdictional entities, this document outlines general principles to assist Forensic Anthropologists in performing their work in an ethical manner. In the absence of specific guidelines or procedures, the principle, spirit, and intent of this code should be met.

Code of Ethics and Conduct

Forensic Anthropologists shall not misrepresent themselves or their work, misappropriate tangible or intellectual property, evade the truth, conspire to deceive, demonstrate disrespect to the dead or their family members, or otherwise betray the confidence placed in them by the public. Specifically, Forensic Anthropologists shall:

1. Treat all human remains with respect and dignity.
2. Respect the privacy and beliefs of the family of the deceased.
3. Treat all evidence with the care and control necessary to ensure its integrity.

4. Comply with all pertinent jurisdictional laws and guidelines regarding the collection, use, and disposition of evidence, particularly those related to human remains.
5. Ensure that all analytical techniques and methods used are appropriate, accurate, and reliable to current scientific standards.
6. Treat all information received from an investigating agency or client with the confidentiality required.
7. Fully and completely disclose all findings to the submitting agency.
8. Testify in a clear, straightforward manner, and refrain from speculation beyond their scope of expertise and professional competence.
9. Ensure that personnel under their direction are appropriately trained and are vetted prior to assisting with anthropological casework.
10. Maintain intellectual independence and impartiality during the analysis of the evidence.
11. Carry out the duties of their profession in such a manner so as to instill the confidence of the public, the forensic science community, and the medicolegal system.
12. Report violations of the Code of Ethics using the appropriate mechanism.
13. Refrain from professional or personal conduct adverse to the best interests of the profession of Forensic Anthropology, including illegal or unethical conduct and the use of their name and credentials in support of illegal or unethical activity.
14. Refrain from misrepresenting their education, training, experience, or expertise.
15. Refrain from knowingly engaging in misrepresenting data upon which expert opinion or conclusion is based. This includes plagiarism, failure to appropriately credit work done by others, falsification of data, falsification of the conditions under which data were obtained, falsification of the results derived from the data, exceeding the limitations of the science, employing unreasonable levels of certainty, or creating false and unreasonable expectations in terms of capability.
16. Avoid actual or apparent undue internal and external political, commercial, financial, and other pressures, influences, and conflicts of interest adversely affecting the quality and integrity of their work.

17. Avoid or disclose involvement in any activities diminishing confidence in their competence, impartiality, independence of judgment, or operational integrity.
18. Refrain from unauthorized data collection.
19. Refrain from extrajudicial statements relating to ongoing investigations except those that a reasonable person would expect to be disseminated by means of public communication. Refrain from unauthorized statements relating to ongoing investigations that do more than state without elaboration the factual and analytical information contained in a public record.
20. Avoid solicitation of work when doing so runs counter to the public interest.
21. Not render services on a contingency fee basis.

SWGANTH GUIDELINE: QUALIFICATIONS

Issue date: Feb 06, 2010

Principle, Spirit, and Intent

Establishing qualifications to practice forensic anthropology ensures that the best interests of the profession, the justice system, and society are served. Practitioners should possess the appropriate qualifications relevant to the forensic anthropology-related duties they are expected to perform.

Purpose and Scope

The following guidelines recommend levels of education, training, experience, and professional activities required to practice forensic anthropology at various levels. These guidelines apply to forensic anthropologists practicing in any laboratory setting including medicolegal facilities, universities, law enforcement agencies, government laboratories, and other crime laboratories.

Laboratories should strive to employ the most qualified forensic anthropologists appropriate to its case-working functions and organizational requirements. Outside the United States, consideration should be given to the availability of comparable education and professional development programs. In the absence of specific guidelines or procedures, the principle, spirit, and intent should be met.

Forensic Anthropologist I

A Forensic Anthropologist I should work under close supervision of a Forensic Anthropologist III. Responsibilities may include data collection (taking measurements and notes), assisting with forensic anthropological analyses, and cosigning reports. A Forensic Anthropologist I should possess the following qualifications:

- A Master's degree (MA or MS) or equivalent in Physical/Biological Anthropology or closely-related field with a significant emphasis on skeletal biology, human variation, human anatomy, and statistics
  OR
- A Bachelor's degree (BA or BS) or equivalent, and active enrollment in a graduate program with a Forensic Anthropologist III with similar emphasis
- Participation in relevant continuing education and training (e.g., workshops, short courses) in forensic anthropology or related fields
- Active membership, at any level, in relevant professional organizations (e.g., American Academy of Forensic Sciences (AAFS), International Association for Identification, American Association of Physical Anthropologists).

Forensic Anthropologist II

A Forensic Anthropologist II independently conducts forensic anthropological analyses and writes and signs reports in a laboratory preferably supervised by a Forensic Anthropologist III. A Forensic Anthropologist II should possess the following qualifications:

- A Master's degree (MA or MS) or equivalent in Physical/Biological Anthropology or closely-related field with a significant emphasis on, human osteology, skeletal biology, human variation, human anatomy, and statistics
- Three years of relevant experience supervised/mentored by a Forensic Anthropologist III, following the previously mentioned degree
- Active certification in forensic anthropology by a Forensic Specialties Accreditation Board-accredited organization (if and when available)
- Participation in relevant continuing education and training (e.g., workshops, short courses) in forensic anthropology or related fields

- Continuing professional development in forensic anthropology including one or more of the following:
  - Conducting research and authoring peer-reviewed publications
  - Professional service
  - Teaching relevant courses at the collegiate level
  - Enrollment in a doctoral program
- Voting membership in the AAFS or comparable organization.

Forensic Anthropologist III

A Forensic Anthropologist III independently conducts forensic anthropological analyses and writes and signs reports. They may be the sole forensic anthropology practitioner in a laboratory, and may supervise individuals at the Forensic Anthropologist I or Forensic Anthropologist II levels. A Forensic Anthropologist III should possess the following qualifications:

- A Doctoral degree (PhD) or equivalent in Physical/Biological Anthropology or closely-related field with a significant emphasis on forensic anthropology, human osteology, skeletal biology, human variation, human anatomy, and statistics
- Three years of sustained, relevant, mentored casework and professional activity, following the previously mentioned degree
- Active certification by the American Board of Forensic Anthropology or other Forensic Specialties Accreditation Board-accredited organization (if and when available)
- Participation in relevant continuing education and training (e.g., workshops, short courses) in forensic anthropology or related fields
- Continuing professional development in forensic anthropology including one or more of the following:
  - Conducting research and authoring peer-reviewed publications
  - Professional service
  - Teaching relevant courses at the collegiate level
- Fellowship in the AAFS or comparable professional organization.

Additional Considerations

A laboratory providing forensic anthropological services or analyses (including sole practitioners/consultants) should have at least one Forensic Anthropologist III in residence who directly supervises the work of individuals at the Forensic Anthropologist I and II levels.

SWGANTH GUIDELINE: EDUCATION AND TRAINING

Issue Date: Jun 13, 2013

Principle, Spirit, and Intent

The profession of forensic anthropology requires education and training that has both breadth in the scope of anthropological inquiry and depth in specific areas of related practice. A holistic understanding of anthropology is fundamental to the practice of forensic anthropology.

Purpose and Scope

This guideline outlines the education and training that should be achieved to practice forensic anthropology. Contrasted with a set curriculum, these guidelines suggest themes and topics designed to provide students and professionals with the basic knowledge and skills required to both meet qualification guidelines (see SWGANTH Qualifications) and practice forensic anthropology. Aspiring practitioners of forensic anthropology should implement these guidelines to the fullest extent as applicable, practical, and appropriate. In the absence of specific guidance or contradictory guidelines, the principle, spirit, and intent should be met.

General Principles

Education should provide a broad background in anthropological theory, methods, and techniques, as well as specialization at the graduate level to include forensic casework experience and a focused research program. Documentation of education and training should be maintained.

The educational and training process should include mentorship and supervision by a practicing Forensic Anthropologist III (see SWGANTH Qualifications). Appropriate education and training in forensic anthropology prepares an individual to pass a certification examination and serve as a practitioner.

Any one practitioner may not necessarily acquire all skills and knowledge in the various fields used in forensic anthropological casework, but should be conversant in all areas. In addition, some positions may require specialized education and training.

Best Practices

The following sections outline specific education and training guidelines.

Education

Undergraduate education should focus on broad, holistic anthropological inquiry, usually attained with an anthropology degree and additional training in the physical and natural sciences. Graduate education should include anthropological theory with an emphasis on human variation and anatomy, skeletal biology, archaeology, and the other primary areas listed later. Students, particularly graduate students, should begin professional activities, such as active student membership within the AAFS, and attend and present at regional and national forensic science meetings. Students are encouraged to gain exposure to other areas of forensic sciences for a broader understanding of the role of forensic anthropology. Students are encouraged to use outside resources to augment their education in forensic anthropology and related sciences (e.g., internships, postgraduate fellowships, short courses).

Students should have university-level coursework in the following primary and secondary areas.

Primary Areas

- Human variation
- Human osteology
- Skeletal pathology
- Evolutionary theory
- Archaeological theory, method, and field work
- Statistics and mathematics
- Research methods and design
- Anthropological theory
- Human growth and development
- Bone biology
- Dental anthropology
- Genetics and molecular biology
- Cultural anthropology
- Human and comparative anatomy and physiology
- General forensic sciences
- Ethics
- Taphonomy

Secondary Areas

- Radiology
- Photography
- Legal procedures
- Evidence handling and security
- Biomechanics
- Bone histology
- Epidemiology

Training

Training outside the classroom is necessary for the successful practice of forensic anthropology. Training should be documented in a training log that is verified by a trainer. Practitioners should receive mentoring from qualified professionals in the following areas:

- Chain of custody procedures
- Laboratory management and quality assurance
- Photographic techniques
- Radiographic techniques
- Microscopy and slide preparation
- Metric analysis including geometric morphometric techniques
- Biological profile methods and techniques
- Trauma analysis
- Personal identification
- Report writing
- Field search and recovery

Supplemental Education

Educational opportunities are available in multiple forms and are not limited to formal course curricula. Supplemental education may be accomplished through the following venues:

- Attendance and active participation at meetings and workshops, and/or presentation of research at professional organizations (e.g., AAFS, International Association for Identification, and American Association of Physical Anthropologists)
- Participation in international initiatives in forensic anthropology
- Studying relevant publications in forensic anthropology and related areas
- Short courses
- Professional seminars and workshops

Guest and invited speakers and lectures
Courses at any advanced education level
Internships/apprenticeships/residencies/fellowships/post-docs
Online seminars through forensic and legal agencies
Research
Professional service
Teaching

Research

Research and publication of findings allows forensic anthropologists to stay abreast of the field as well as fill gaps and deficiencies in previous knowledge. Research should be published in peer-reviewed venues.

Unacceptable Practices

The following practices are considered unacceptable and should be avoided:

Falsely representing training and experience
Failing to maintain current and accurate records of education, training, or certification.

APPENDIX C

Websites of Ethical Codes (Accessed November 2017)

National code of ethics and professional responsibility for the forensic sciences

https://www.justice.gov/archives/ncfs/page/file/788576/download

AAFS Code of Ethics and Conduct

https://www.aafs.org/aafs-ethics/

ABFA Policies and Procedures (to include Code of Ethics and Conduct (2016 Revision))

http://theabfa.org/wp-content/uploads/2017/06/ABFA-Policies-and-Procedures.pdf

AAPA ethics committee

https://www.aafs.org/aafs-ethics/

Society of Forensic Anthropologists—Ethics

http://www.sofainc.org/code-of-ethics

American Anthropological Association—Code of Ethics

http://s3.amazonaws.com/rdcms-aaa/files/production/public/FileDownloads/pdfs/issues/policy-advocacy/upload/ethicscode.pdf

National Association for the Practice of Anthropology—Ethical Guidelines

http://practicinganthropology.org/about/ethical-guidelines/

Society for American Archaeology—Principles of Archaeological Ethics http://www.saa.org/AbouttheSociety/PrinciplesofArchaeologicalEthics/tabid/203/Default.aspx

British Association for Forensic Anthropology—Draft Code of Practice for Forensic Anthropology

https://www.gov.uk/government/consultations/code-of-practice-for-forensic-anthropology

Chartered Institute for Archaeologists Code of Conduct

https://www.archaeologists.net/sites/default/files/CodesofConduct.pdf

British Association of Biological Anthropology and Osteoarchaeology Code of Ethics

http://www.babao.org.uk/assets/Uploads/code-of-ethics.pdf

REFERENCES

ANAB, 2017. ISO/IEC 17025:2005 – Forensic Science Testing Laboratories: Accreditation Requirements. ANAB, Effective: 2017/06/01.

Alberti, S.J.M.M., Bienkowski, P., Chapman, M.J., Drew, R., 2009. Should we display the dead? Mus. Soc. 7 (3), 133–149.

Alberti, S.J.M.M., Bienkowski, P., Chapman, M.J., Drew, R., 2015. Should we display the dead? Mus. Soc. 7 (3), 17.

American Restatement (Second) of Torts: Interference with Dead Bodies § 868. 1979. American Law Institute.

Annas, G.J., Grodin, M.A., 1992. Introduction. In: Annas, G.J., Grodin, M.A. (Eds.), The Nazi Doctors and the Nuremberg Code. Oxford University Press, New York, pp. 3–11.

Appelbaum, P.S., 1997. A theory of ethics for forensic psychiatry. J. Am. Acad. Psychiatry Law 25, 233–248.

Appelbaum, P.S., 2008. Ethics and forensic psychiatry: translating principles into practice. J. Am. Acad. Psychiatry Law 36 (2), 195.

Assembly, U.G., 1948. Universal Declaration of Human Rights. UN General Assembly.

Attfield, R., 2012. Ethics: An Overview. Continuum International Publishing, London.

Badgett, M.V.L., Durso, L.E., Kastanis, A., Mallory, C., 2013. The Buisness Impact of LGBT-Supportive Workplace Policies. The Williams Institute.

Balter, M., 2016. The sexual misconduct case that has rocked anthropology. Science, http://doi.org/10.1126/science.aaf4016.

Barnett, P.D., 2001. Ethics in Forensic Science: Professional Standards for the Practice of Criminalistics. CRC Press, Boca Raton, FL.

Beede, D.N., Julian, T.A., Langdon, D., McKittrick, G., Khan, B., Doms, M.E., 2011. Women in STEM: a gender gap to innovation. Econ. Stat. Adm. Issue Brief No. 04-11: Available at SSRN: https://ssrn.com/abstract = 1964782 or https://doi.org/1964710.1962139/ssrn.1964782.

Benos, D.J., Bashari, E., Chaves, J.M., Gaggar, A., Kapoor, N., LaFrance, M., et al., 2007. The ups and downs of peer review. Adv. Physiol. Educ. 31 (2), 145–152.

Berger, R.L., 1990. Nazi science—the Dachau hypothermia experiments. New Engl. J. Med. 322 (20), 1435–1440.

Berkenkotter, C., 1995. The power and the perils of peer review. Rhetor. Rev. 13 (2), 245–248.

Berryman, H.E., Lanfear, A.K., 2012. Forensic anthropologists in medical examiner's and coroner's offices: a history. In: Dirkmaat, D. (Ed.), A Companion to Forensic Anthropology. John Wiley & Sons, Ltd, Malden, MA, pp. 534–548.

Berryman, H.E., Bass, W.M., Symes, S.A., Smith, O.C., 1991. Recognition of cemetery remains in the forensic setting. J Forensic Sci 36 (1), 230–237.

Berryman, H.E., Bass, W.M., Symes, S.A., Smith, O.B.C., 1997. Recognition of Cemetery Remains in the Forensic Setting. In: Haglund, W.D., Sorg, M.H. (Eds.), Forensic Taphonomy: The Postmortem Fate of Human Remains. CRC Press, NY, pp. 165–170.

Bethard, J.D., 2016. Historical trends in graduate research and training of Diplomates of the American Board of Forensic Anthropology. J. Forensic Sci. 62 (1), 5–11.

Bird, C.E., 2016. Population bias and its advantages in forensic anthropological casework. Program of American Association of Physical Anthropologists Supplement, p. 97.

Bird, C.E., Sykes, J.D., Bird, J.D.P., 2017. The role of stigma in the medicolegal investigation of unidentified persons. In: Proceedings of the American Academy of Forensic Sciences 69th Annual Scientific Meeting, pp. 233–234.

Birkby, W.H., Fenton, T.W., Anderson, B.E., 2008. Identifying Southwest Hispanics using non-metric traits and the cultural profile. J. Forensic Sci. 53 (1), 29–33.

Blacksher, E., Moreno, J.D., 2008. A history of informed consent in clinical research. In: Emanuel, E.J., Grady, C., Crouch, R.A., Lie, R.K., Miller, F.G., Wendler, D. (Eds.), The Oxford Textbook of Clinical Research Ethics. Oxford University Press, Oxford, pp. 591–605.

Blumenbach, J.F., 1775. De generis humani varietate nativa liber [On the Natural Variety of Mankind]. Vandenhoek et Ruprecht, Goettingae.

Bono, J., Sweinton, A.R., Downs, J.C.U., 2012. Ethics in testimony. In: Downs, J.U., Swienton, A.R. (Eds.), Ethics in Forensic Science. Academic Press, San Diego, pp. 343–376.

Bowen, R.T., 2009. Ethics and the Practice of Forensic Science. CRC Press, Boca Raton, FL.

Brian, W., Meehan, V., American Media International, LLC. 2011. North Carolina Court of Appeals.

Briody, E.K., Pester, T.M., 2014. The coming of age of anthropological practice and ethics. J. Bus. Anthropol. 1 (1), 11–37.

Brodkin, K., Morgen, S., Hutchinson, J., 2011. Anthropology as white public space? Am. Anthropol 113 (4), 545–556.

Brown, C., 2010. Revisiting McKern and Stewart (1957): a comparison of pubic symphysis methods at the JPAC/CIL. In: Latham, K.A., Finnegan, M. (Eds.), Age Estimations of the Human Skeleton. Charles C. Thomas, Springfield, Illinois, pp. 161–176.

Burke, K.L., 2012. Schmorl's nodes in an American military population: frequency, formation, and etiology. J. Forensic Sci. 57 (3), 571–577.

Caplan, A., 2011. The use of prisoners as sources of organs–an ethically dubious practice. Am. J. Bioeth. 11 (10), 1–5.

Ceci, S.J., Williams, W.M., 2011. Understanding current causes of women's underrepresentation in science. Proc. Natl. Acad. Sci. 108 (8), 3157–3162.

Champney, T.H., 2016. The business of bodies: ethical perspectives on for-profit body donation companies. Clin. Anat. 29 (1), 25–29.

Childress, J.F., 2017. Reflections on the National Bioethics Advisory Commission and Models of Public Bioethics. Hastings Cent. Rep. 47 (Suppl 1), S20–S23.

Christensen, A.M., Crowder, C.M., 2009. Evidentiary standards for forensic anthropology. J. Forensic Sci. 54 (6), 1211–1216.

Christensen, A.M., Passalacqua, N.V., Bartelink, E.J., 2014. Forensic Anthropology: Current Methods and Practice. Elsevier, San Diego, CA.

Cicchetti, D.V., 1997. Referees, editors, and publication practices: improving the reliability and usefulness of the peer review system. Sci. Eng. Ethics 3 (1), 51–62.

Clancy, K.B.H., Nelson, R.G., Rutherford, J.N., Hinde, K., 2014. Survey of Academic Field Experiences (SAFE): trainees report harassment and assault. PLoS One 9 (7), e102172.

Conger, D., Long, M.C., 2010. Why are men falling behind? Gender gaps in college performance and persistence. Ann. Am. Acad. Pol. Soc. Sci. 627 (1), 184–214.

Consoli, L., 2006. Scientific misconduct and science ethics: a case study based approach. Sci. Eng. Ethics 12, 533–541.

Cooley, C.M., 2004. Reforming the forensic science community to avert the ultimate injustice. Stan. L. Pol. Rev. 15 (2), 381–446.

Cooper, J., Neuhaus, I.M., 2000. The "Hired Gun" effect: assessing the effect of pay, frequency of testifying, and credentials on the perception of expert testimony. Law Hum. Behav. 24 (2), 149–171.

DPAA Laboratory Manual, 2017. SOP 4.0: CIL Surety. Last Revised: 30 March 2017.

Dasgupta, N., 2004. Unclaimed bodies at the anatomy table. JAMA 291 (1), 122–123.

Denton, J.S., 2013. Ethics education in forensic pathology fellowship training: Is there a need? Acad. Forensic Pathol. 3 (3), 312–316.

Department for Culture Media and Sport: London, 2005. Guidance for the Care of Human Remains in Museums.

Donlon, D., 2016. The development and current state of forensic anthropogy: an Australian perspective. In: Blau, S., Ubelaker, D.H. (Eds.), Handbook of Forensic Anthropology and Archaeology. Routledge, New York, pp. 126–139.

Epstein, J., 2017. Forensic laboratory reports. In: Houck, M.M. (Ed.), Forensic Anthropology. Elsevier, San Diego, pp. 377–380.

Fforde, C., 2014. Tamaki Makau-Rau Accord on the display of human remains and sacred objects (2005). In: Smith, C. (Ed.), Encyclopedia of Global Archaeology. Springer, New York, New York, NY, pp. 7209–7213.

Fluehr-Lobban, C., 2003. Ethics and anthropology 1890-2000: a review of issues and principles. In: Fluehr-Lobban, C. (Ed.), Ethics and the Profession of Anthropology: Dialogue for Ethically Conscious Practice. Alta-Mira Press, Walnut Creek, CA, pp. 1–28.

Fowler, G., Hughes, C., 2017. Development and assessment of postcranial sex estimation methods for a Guatemalan population. J. Forensic Science. Available from: http://doi.org/10.1111/1556-4029.13570.

France, D.L., 2012. Ethics in forensic anthropology. In: Dirkmaat, D. (Ed.), A Companion to Forensic Anthropology. John Wiley & Sons, Ltd, Malden, MA, pp. 666–682.

Frutos, L.R., 2003. Brief communication: Sex determination accuracy of the minimum supero-inferior femoral neck diameter in a contemporary rural Guatemalan population. Am. J. Phys. Anthropol. 122 (2), 123–126.

Giunta, L.A., 2010. The dead on display: a call for the international regulation of plastination exhibits. Colum. J. Transnat'l L. 49 (1), 164–194.

Glantz, L.H., 1992. The influence of the Nuremberg Code on U.S. statutes and regulations. In: Annas, G.J., Grodin, M.A. (Eds.), The Nazi Doctors and the Nuremberg Code. Oxford University Press, New York, pp. 183–200.

Goodman, S.N., Berlin, J., Fletcher, S.W., Fletcher, R.H., 1994. Manuscript quality before and after peer review and editing at Annals of Internal Medicine. Ann. Intern. Med. 121 (1), 11–21.

Grivas, C.R., Komar, D.A., 2008. Kumho, Daubert, and the nature of scientific inquiry: implications for forensic anthropology. J. Forensic Sci. 53 (4), 771–776.

Guffey, M.E., Almonte, R., 2010. Essentials of Business Communication. Nelson Education, Toronto.

Haden-Pinneri, K., Weedn, V.W., 2013. Organ and tissue retention. Acad. Forensic Pathol. 3 (3), 294–300.

Henderson, C., Lenz, K.W., 2015. Expert witness qualifications and testimony. In: Houck, M.M. (Ed.), Professional Issues in Forensic Science. Academic Press, San Diego, pp. 281–284.

Henneberg, M., 2016. The expert witness and the court of law. In: Blau, S., Ubelaker, D.H. (Eds.), Handbook of Forensic Anthropology and Archaeology. Routledge, New York, pp. 635–641.

Holland, T.D., 2015. “Since I must please those below”: human skeletal remains research and the law. Am. J. L. Med. 41 (4), 617–655.

Holland, T.D., Byrd, J., Sava, V., 2008. Joint POW/MIA Accounting Command's Central Idenfitifcation Laboratory. In: Warren, M.W., Walsh-Haney, H.A., Freas, L.E. (Eds.), The Forensic Anthropology Laboratory. CRC Press, Boca Raton, FL, pp. 47–63.

Houck, M.M., 2009. Is forensic science a gateway for women in science? Forensic Sci. Pol. Manag.: Int. J. 1 (1), 65–69.

Hubbard, A.R., 2017. Teaching race (bioculturally) matters: a visual approach for college biology courses. Am. Biol. Teacher 79 (7), 516–524.

ICRC, 2003. The Missing and Their Families. Geneva.

Jones, D.G., Whitaker, M.I., 2012. Anatomy's use of unclaimed bodies. Clin. Anat. 25 (2), 246–254.

Joy, J., 2017. Looking death in the face: different attitutdes towards bog bodies and their display with a focus on Lindow Man. In: Fletcher, A., Antoine, D. (Eds.), Regarding the Dead: Human Remains in the British Museum. British Museum Press, London, pp. 10–19.

Kalev, A., Dobbin, F., Kelly, E., 2006. Best Practices or Best Guesses? Assessing the efficacy of corporate affirmative action and diversity policies. Am. Sociol. Rev. 71 (4), 589–617.

Kaye, D.H., 2010. The good, the bad, the ugly: the NAS report on strengthening forensic science in America. Sci. Justice 50, 8–11.

Kimmerle, E.H., Baraybar, J.P. (Eds.), 2008. Skeletal Trauma: Identification of Injuries Resulting from Human Rights Abuse and Armed Conflict. CRC Press, Boca Raton, FL.

Kimmerle, E.H., Konigsberg, L.W., Jantz, R.L., Baraybar, J.P., 2008. Analysis of age-at-death estimation through the use of pubic symphyseal data. J. Forensic Sci. 53, 558–568.

Klales, A.R., Ousley, S.D., Vollner, J.M., 2012. A revised method of sexing the human innominate using Phenice's nonmetric traits and statistical methods. Am. J. Phys. Anthropol. 149 (1), 104–114.

Konigsberg, L.W., Herrmann, N.P., Wescott, D.J., Kimmerle, E.H., 2008. Estimation and evidence in forensic anthropology: age-at-death. J. Forensic Sci. 53 (3), 541–557.

Koppl, R., 2005. How to improve forensic science. Eur. J. Law Econ. 20 (3), 255–286.

Kramer, M.H., 2015. Do animals and dead people have legal rights? Can. J. Law Jurisprud. 14 (1), 29–54.

Krimsky, S., 2006. Publication, bias, data owndership, and the Funding Effect in science: Threats to the integrity of biomedical research. In: Wagner, R., Steinzor, R. (Eds.), Rescuing Science from Politics: Regulation and the Distortion of Scientific Research. Cambridge University Press, New York, pp. 61–85.

Krimsky, S., 2010. Combating the funding effect in science: what's beyond transparency. Stan. Law Pol. Rev. 21 (1), 101–123.

Langley, N.R., Tersigni-Tarrant, M. (Eds.), 2017. Forensic Anthropology: A Comprehensive Introduction. CRC Press, Boca Raton, FL.

Larsen, C.S., Walker, P.L., 2005. The ethics of bioarchaeology. In: Turner, T.R. (Ed.), Biological Anthropology and Ethics: From Repatriation to Genetic Identity. State University of New York Press, Albany, pp. 111–119.

Lesciotto, K.M., 2015. The impact of Daubert on the admissibility of forensic anthropology expert testimony. J. Forensic Sci. 60 (3), 549–555.

Luzi, S.A., Melinek, J., Oliver, W.R., 2013. Medical examiner's independence is vital for the health of the American legal system. Acad. Forensic Pathol. 3 (1), 84–92.

Manghani, K., 2011. Quality assurance: importance of systems and standard operating procedures. Perspect. Clin. Res. 2 (1), 34–37.

Marquez-Grant, N., Fibiger, L. (Eds.), 2011. The Routledge Handbook of Arhcaoelogical Human Remains and Legislation. Routledge Handbooks, London.

McKern, T., Stewart, T.D., 1957. Skeletal changes in young American males. Quartermaster Research and Development Command Technical Report EP-45, Natick, MA.

Meadows Jantz, L., 2013. Processing and inventory of remains. In: Tersigni-Tarrant, M.A., Shirley, N.R. (Eds.), Forensic Anthropology: An Introduction. CRC Press, Boca Raton, FL, pp. 121–137.

Melinek, J., Thomas, L.C., Oliver, W.R., Schmunk, G.A., Weedn, V.W., 2013. National Association of Medical Examiners position paper: medical examiner, coroner, and forensic pahtologist independence. Acad. Forensic Pathol. 3 (1), 93–988.

Menikoff, J., Kaneshiro, J., Pritchard, I., 2017. The common rule, updated. New Engl. J. Med. 376 (7), 613–615.

Merriam-Webster's Dictionary of Law, 1996a. Discriminate. Merriam-Webster's Dictionary of Law. Merriam-Webster, Incorporated, Springfield, Massachusetts, p. 142.

Merriam-Webster's Dictionary of Law, 1996b. Harass. Merriam-Webster's Dictionary of Law. Merriam-Webster, Incorporated, Springfield, Massachusetts, p. 222.

Milkman, K.L., Akinola, M., Chugh, D., 2015. What happens before? A field experiment exploring how pay and representation differentially shape bias on the pathway into organizations. J. Appl. Psychol. 100 (6), 1678.

Mnookin, J., Cole, S.A., Dror, I., Fisher, B.A., Houk, M., Inman, K., et al., 2011. The need for a research culture in the forensic sciences. UCLA Law Rev 58, 725–780.

Moe, K., 1984. Should the Nazi research data be cited? Hastings Cent. Rep. 14 (6), 5–7.

Morton, S.G., 1839. Crania Americana. J. Dobson, Philadelphia.

Morton, S.G., 1844. Crania Aegyptica. John Penington, Philadelphia.

Mosteller, R.P., 2008. Exculpatory evidence, ethics and the road to the disbarment of Mike Nifong: The critical importance of full open-file discovery. George Mason Law Rev. 15 (2), 257–318.

Mostow, P., 2015. "Like Building on Top of Auschwitz": on the symbolic meaning of using data from the Nazi experiments, and on non-use as a form of memorial. J. Law Relig. 10 (2), 403–431.

Murphy, J.P., 2000. Expert witnesses at trial: where are the ethics? Geo. J. Legal Ethics 14, 217–239.

Murray, E., Anderson, B., 2007. Forensic anthropology in the courtroom: trends in testimony. In: Proceedings of the Annual Meeting of the American Academy of Forensic Sciences, pp. 322–333.

Murrie, D.C., Boccaccini, M.T., Guarnera, L.A., Rufino, K.A., 2013. Are forensic experts biased by the side that retained them? Psychol. Sci. Available from: https://doi.org/10.1177/0956797613481812.

NSF, 2017. Women, Minorities, and Persons with Disabilities in Science and Engineering.

Nakhaeizadeh, S., Dror, I.E., Morgan, R.M., 2014a. Cognitive bias in forensic anthropology: visual assessment of skeletal remains is susceptible to confirmation bias. Sci. Justice 54 (3), 208–214.

Nakhaeizadeh, S., Hanson, I., Dozzi, N., 2014b. The power of contextual effects in forensicaAnthropology: a study of biasability in the visual interpretations of trauma analysis on skeletal remains. J. Forensic Sci. 59 (5), 1177–1183.

National Bioethics Advisory Committee, 1999. Research Involving Human Biological Materials: Ethical Issues and Policy Guidance. Rockville, Maryland. Available from: https://bioethicsarchive.georgetown.edu/nbac/hbm.pdf.

National Research Council, 2009. Strengthening Forensic Science in the United States: A Path Forward. National Academy Press, Washington, D.C.

Nelkin, D., Andrews, L., 1998. Do the dead have interests-policy issues for research after life. Am. J. Law Med. 24, 261.

Nelson, R.G., Rutherford, J.N., Hinde, K., Clancy, K.B.H., 2017. Signaling safety: characterizing fieldwork experiences and their implications for career trajectories. Am. Anthropol. Available from: https://doi.org/10.1111/aman.12929.

Nwabueze, R.N., 2007. Biotechnology and the Challenge of Property. Ashgate Publishing Company, Burlington, VT.

Nystrom, K.C., 2014. The bioarchaeology of structural violence and dissection in the 19th century United States. Am. Anthropol. 116 (4), 765–779.

Ottaviano, G.I.P., Peri, G., 2006. The economic value of cultural diversity: evidence from US cities. J. Econ. Geo. 6 (1), 9–44.

Panofsky, A., Donovan, J., 2017. When genetics challenges a racist's identity: genetic ancestry testing among white nationalists. SocArXiv osf.io/preprints/socarxiv/7f9bc(August 17).

Paolello, J.M., Klales, A.R., 2014. Contemporary cultural alterations to bone. In: Pokines, J.T., Symes, S.A. (Eds.), Manual of Forensic Taphonomy. CRC Press, Boca Raton, Fl, pp. 181–200.

Parker, L.S., London, A.J., Aronson, J.D., 2013. Incidental findings in the use of DNA to identify human remains: an ethical assessment. Forensic Sci. Int.: Genet. 7 (2), 221–229.

Passalacqua, N.V., Pilloud, M.A., Gruters, G.A., 2014. Letter to the Editor—Professionalism: ethics and scholarship in forensic science. J. Forensic Sci. 59 (2), 573–575.

Pellegrino, E.D., 2002. Professionalism, profession and the virtues of the good physician. Mount Sinai J. Med. 69 (6), 378.

Pentz, R.D., 2005. Ethics guidelines for research with the recently dead. Nat. Med. 11, 1145–1149.

Perley, S., Fluss, S.S., Bankowski, Z., Simon, F., 1992. The Nuremberg Code: an international overiew. In: Annas, G.J., Grodin, M.A. (Eds.), The Nazi Doctors and the Nuremberg Code. Oxford University Press, New York, pp. 149–173.

Peterson, G.F., Clark, S.C., 2006. Forensic autopsy performance standards. Am. J. Forensic Med. Pathol. 27 (3), 200–225.

Pilloud, M.A., Tersigni-Tarrant, M., 2017. Remains as evidence. In: Tersigni-Tarrant, M. (Ed.), Forensic Anthropology: A Comprehensive Introduction. CRC Press, Boca Raton, Fl, pp. 23–33.

Popper, K., 1963. Conjecture and Refutations. Basic Books, New York.

Porter, J.P., Koski, G., 2008. Regulations for the protection of humans in research in the United States: the common rule. In: Emanuel, E.J., Grady, C., Crouch, R.A., Lie, R.K., Miller, F.G., Wendler, D. (Eds.), The Oxford Textbook of Clinical Research Ethics. Oxford University Press, Oxford, pp. 156–167.

Pozos, R.S., 2003. Nazi hypothermia research: should the data be used? In: Beam, T.E., Sparacino, L.R. (Eds.), Military Medical Ethics. Office of the Surgeon General, Washington DC, pp. 437–461.

President's Committee of Advisors on Science and Technology Panel on Educational Technology, 2016. Report to the President Forensic Science in Criminal Courts: Ensuring Scientific Validity of Feature-Comparison Methods.

Redfern, R., Clegg, M., 2017. Archaeologically derived human remains in England: legacy and future. World Archaeol. 1–14. Available from: https://doi.org/10.1080/00438243.2017.1357494.

Rennie, D., 1999. Editorial peer review: its development and rationale. In: Godlee, F., Jefferson, T. (Eds.), Peer Review in Health Sciences. BMJ Books, London, pp. 1–13.

Rocca, K.A., 2010. Student participation in the college classroom: an extended multidisciplinary literature review. Commun. Educ. 59 (2), 185–213.

Rogers, T.L., 2005. Recognition of cemetery remains in a forensic context. J. Forensic Sci. 50 (1), 5–11.

Rose, J.C., Green, T.J., Green, V.D., 1996. NAGRPA is forever: osteology and the repatriation of skeletons. Annu. Rev. Anthropol. 25, 81–103.

Ross, A.H., Konigsberg, L.W., 2002. New formulae for estimating stature in the Balkans. J. Forensic Sci. 47 (1), 165–167.

Roth, A., 2012. Ethical duties of attorneys and experts in forensic cases. In: Downs, J.U., Swienton, A.R. (Eds.), Ethics in Forensic Science. Academic Press, San Diego, pp. 313–342.

SWGAnth, 2010. Qualifications.

SWGAnth, 2012. Documentation, Reporting and Testimony.

SWGAnth, 2013a. Code of Ethics and Conduct.

SWGAnth, 2013b. Education and Training.

Saxena, A., 2014. Workforce diversity: a key to improve productivity. Proc. Econ. Fin. 11 (Supplement C), 76–85.

Schaefer, M.C., 2008. A summary of epiphyseal union timings in Bosnian males. Int. J. Osteoarchaeol. 18, 536–545.

Schaefer, M.C., Black, S.M., 2005. Comparison of ages of epiphyseal union in North American and Bosnian skeletal material. J. Forensic Sci. 50 (4), 777–784.

Settles, I.H., Cortina, L.M., Malley, J., Stewart, A.J., 2006. The climate for women in academic science: the good, the bad, and the changeable. Psychol. Women Q 30 (1), 47–58.

Shen, H., 2015. Scientific groups revisit sexual-harassment policies. Nature. Available from: https://doi.org/10.1038/nature.2015.18790. News 16 November.

Shuman, D.W., Greenberg, S.A., 2003. The expert witness, the adversary system, and the voice of reason: Reconciling impartiality and advocacy. Prof. Psychol. Res. Prac. 34 (3), 219–224.

Sitch, B., 2010. Courting controversy - the Lindow Man exhibition at the Manchester Museum. International Committee for University Museums and Collections (UMAC).

Sledzik, P.S., Micozzi, M.S., 1997. Autopsied, embalmed, and preserved human remains: distinguishing features in forensic and historic contexts. In: Haglund, W.D., Sorg, M.H. (Eds.), Forensic Taphonomy: The Postmortem Fate of Human Remains. CRC Press, Boca Raton, pp. 483–495.

Smith, R., 1997. Peer review: reform or revolution? BMJ 315, 759–760.

Sperling, D., 2008. Posthumous Interests: Legal and Ethical Perspectives. Cambridge University Press, Cambridge.

Sun, L., 2016. How American hates socialism without knowing why. <http://evonomics.com/america-hates-socialism-without-knowing>.

Sun, M., 1988. EPA bars use of Nazi data. Science 240, 21.

Ta'ala, S.C., Berg, G.E., Haden, K., 2006. Blunt force cranial trauma in the Cambodian killing fields. J. Forensic Sci. 51, 996–1001.

Taverniers, I., De Loose, M., Van Bockstaele, E., 2004. Trends in quality in the analytical laboratory. II. Analytical method validation and quality assurance. TrAC Trends Anal. Chem. 23 (8), 535–552.

The National Commission for the Protection of Human Subjects of Biomedical and Behavioral Research, 1978. The Belmont Report: Ethical Principles and Guidelines for the Protection of Human Subjects of Research. US Government Printing Office, Bethesda, MD.

Thurner, S., Hanel, R., 2011. Peer-review in a world with rational scientists: toward selection of the average. Eur. Phys. J. B 84 (4), 707–711.

Trials of War Criminals Before the Nuernberg Military Tribunals under Control Council Law No. 10, Volume II, 1949. U.S. Government Printing Office, Washington, D.C.

Trotter, M., Gleser, G.C., 1952. Estimation of stature from long bones of American Whites and Negroes. Am. J. Phys. Anthropol. 10, 463–514.

Trotter, R.T., 2009. Formalizing ethics training in anthropology: an extension of methods education. Anthropol. News 50 (6), 32–33.

Ubelaker, D.H., 2011. United States of America. In: Marquez-Grant, N., Fibiger, L. (Eds.), The Routledge Handbook of Archaeological Human Remains and Legislation. Routledge Handbooks, New York, pp. 533–540.

Ubelaker, D.H., 2016. The dynamic interface of bioarchaeology and forensic anthropology. Intersecciones en Antropología 17 (2), 5–38.

Wagner, J.K., Yu, J.-H., Ifekwunigwe, J.O., Harrell, T.M., Bamshad, M.J., Royal, C.D., 2017. Anthropologists' views on race, ancestry, and genetics. Am. J. Phys. Anthropol. 162 (2), 318–327.

Walker, P.L., 2008. Bioarchaeological ethics: a historical perpective on the value of human remains. In: Katzenberg, A., Saunders, S. (Eds.), Biological Anthropology of the Human Skeleton. Wily-Liss, Wilimington, pp. 3–39.

Walsh-Haney, H.A., Lieberman, L.S., 2005. Ethical concerns in forensic anthropology. In: Turner, T. (Ed.), Biological Anthropology and Ethics: From Repatriation to Genetic Identity. State University of New York Press, Albany, Albany, New York, pp. 121–132.

Warner, T.D., Weiss, R.L., 2004. Scientific integrity, fidelity and conflicts of interest. Curr. Opin. Psychiatry 17 (5), 381–385.

Weitzman, M., 1990. The ethics of using Nazi medical data: a Jewish perspective. Second Opin. 14, 26–38 (Park Ridge, Ill).

Wells, A.S., Fox, L., Cordova-Cobo, D., 2016. How racially diverse schools and classrooms can benefit all students. Educ. Dig. 82 (1), 17–24.

Wicclair, M.R., DeVita, M., 2004. Oversight of research involving the dead. Kennedy Inst. Ethics J. 14 (2), 143–156.

Williams, A., 2011. Femme Fatales: Why do women dominate the discipline of forensic anthropology. In: Proceedings of the American Academy of Forensic Sciences Annual Scientific Meeting, pp. 337–338.

Williams, J.E., 2016. Decoding Racial Ideology in Genomics. Lexington Books, Lanham, Maryland.

Willoughby, F.W., Thompson, E., Downs, J.C.U., 2012. The forensic practitioner's quest for the truth. In: Downs, J.C.U., Swienton, A.R. (Eds.), Ethics in Forensic Science. Academic Press, San Diego, pp. 27–57.

Wolf, S.M., 2008. Introduction: the challenge of incidental findings. J. Law Med. Ethics 36 (2), 216–218.

Wolf, S.M., Lawrenz, F.P., Nelson, C.A., Kahn, J.P., Cho, M.K., Clayton, E.W., et al., 2008. Managing incidental findings in human subjects research: analysis and recommendations. J. Law Med. Ethics 36 (2), 219–248.

Wolft, L.D., 2005. Field primatologists: duties, rights, and obligations. In: Turner, T. (Ed.), Biological Anthropology and Ethics: From Repatriation to Genetic Identity. SUNY Press, Albany, New York, pp. 15–26.

World Medical Association, 2013. World Medical Association Declaration of Helsinki: ethical principles for medical research involving human subjects. J. Am. Med. Assoc. 310 (20), 2191–2194.

General Assembly of the World Medical Association, 2014. World Medical Association Declaration of Helsinki: ethical principles for medical research involving human subjects. J. Am. Coll. Dent. 81 (3), 14–18.

Wright, L.E., Vasquez, M.A., 2003. Estimating the length of incomplete long bones: forensic standards from Guatemala. Am. J. Phys. Anthropol. 120 (3), 233–251.

Yasko, L.L., Wicclair, M., DeVita, M.A., 2004. Committee for Oversight of Research Involving the Dead (CORID): insights from the first year. Camb. Q Healthc. Ethics 13 (4), 327–337.

Zuckerman, M.K., Kamnikar, K.R., Mathena, S.A., 2014. Recovering the 'Body Politic': a relational ethics of meaning for bioarchaeology. Camb. Archaeol. J. 24, 513–522.

INDEX